Great
Michigan
Deer Tales

Doug,
Best of luck,
Deer Hunting!

Richard P. Smith

Great
Michigan
Deer Tales

Stories Behind
Michigan's Biggest Bucks

Richard P. Smith

Smith Publications

Great Michigan Deer Tales
Stories Behind Michigan's Biggest Bucks

by Richard P. Smith

Published by:
Smith Publications
814 Clark St.
Marquette, MI 49855

All photos by the author unless otherwise credited
Cover photo by Richard P. Smith
Cover design by Robert Howard
Book production by Lucy Smith
Interior layout and design by Kay Richey
Electronically created camera-ready copy by:
KLR Communications, Inc.
POB 192
Grawn, MI 49637

Printed on recycled paper

Library of Congress Cataloging in Publication Data
Smith, Richard P.
Great Michigan Deer Tales: Stories Behind Michigan's Biggest Bucks / by Richard P. Smith
Deer hunting—Michigan
SK 301.S6 1994   799.27SM   94-067255
ISBN 0-9617407-5-2 Softcover

For Lucy
who sometimes listens to
more deer tales than she would like to!

Contents

Acknowledgments

First and foremost I would like to acknowledge and thank all officers and measurers, past and present, of Commemorative Bucks of Michigan (CBM) for their efforts in measuring many of the big antlered bucks bagged in the state each year and for maintaining a dependable set of records that are becoming an increasingly valuable reference for all big game hunters interested in trying their luck in Michigan. These records help promote the state and give it the credit that's due as one of this country's best whitetail producers. Through the help of CBM I have been able to locate and interview some of the hunters mentioned in this book.

CBM's records are referred to frequently in the pages that follow to help put the size of the racks that are discussed in perspective. How the antlers rank in the county where they were taken and on a statewide basis is mentioned in most, if not all, cases.

Hunters do not have to have bagged a buck or any other trophy animal that qualifies for state records to belong to CBM. Annual memberships are $15. To join, send a check or money order to CBM, 3215 Old Farm Lane, Walled Lake, MI 48390. For additional information call 810-796-2925.

A list of CBM's statewide network of scorers, along with their addresses and telephone numbers, should be available at most DNR offices.

Contact the CBM representative nearest to you to make an appointment to have your antlers measured. All racks must air dry for 60 days before they can be officially scored. The deadline for each year's scoring period is March 31. There's a $5 charge to enter antlers in state records that meet minimum qualifications for hunters who do not belong to the organization. Members can enter as many as they wish at no charge.

I also want to publicly thank all of the deer hunters who have shared their tales with me so I could write about them and allowed me the opportunity to photograph their trophy bucks. I never tire of hearing exciting deer tales, especially those dealing with big bucks, and seeing the trophy animals. An even bigger thanks goes out to family and friends who I have hunted with, sharing deer tales on another level.

Current and former DNR wildlife biologists deserve credit for doing their best to manage the state's whitetail population in spite of interference from well meaning hunters who are often poorly informed and politicians who frequently have interests other than the welfare of our deer herd in mind. Conservation officers deserve a pat on the back, too, for doing what they can to protect deer from poachers.

Kay Richey, wife of longtime friend and fellow outdoor writer Dave Richey, was generous in providing advice as well as doing the typesetting and layout for this book. Your assistance was greatly appreciated Kay. Thanks!

My wife Lucy deserves special credit as my business partner who took care of many of the important details and work required to complete this book and to get it into your hands. Her skill and foresight went into selecting the computer this book was produced on as well as in many other ways so I can concentrate on one of my life's most important activities - DEER HUNTING!

Introduction

If you like reading about BIG BUCKS and the hunters who took them, you will want to read this book. It contains more solid information about more of Michigan's most memorable bucks and some of the state's best deer hunters than any book previously published. Learn how, where and when some of the state's biggest bucks were bagged with rifle, shotgun, handgun, muzzleloader and bow and arrow.

If you are interested in bagging a BOOK BUCK in Michigan yourself, studying this collection of success stories will help make it happen. There's no better way to learn than from those who have already accomplished the feat, some of whom have done it over and over again. The detailed accounts in this book will eliminate some of the mystery surrounding what it takes to collect some of the biggest bucks that have ever lived in the state. You might be surprised at how similar many of the elements are, at least those that hunters have control over, in each of these success stories.

Although most of this book's contents is devoted to bucks with huge racks and the hunters who tagged them, there are also chapters on some of the state's heaviest and oldest whitetails, both bucks and does. The chapters in this book are not only intended to educate, they are also entertaining. Detailed descriptions and quotes from hunters will enable you to share the exhilaration and excitement they felt when they saw and shot the biggest bucks of their lives. You will be able to relive those precious moments as though you were there with them.

You will read about special deer hunts enjoyed by families and friends in addition to dedicated individuals. You will find out how skill, luck, fate, dedication, persistence and various hunting techniques played important roles in these unique tales about deer hunting. These hunts took place during each of the state's deer seasons and in every region of the state and that's one of the reasons they were selected for inclusion in this book.

This book was put together at this time to help commemorate 100 years of licensed deer hunting in Michigan. The first year that deer hunters in the state were required to buy licenses to hunt whitetails was 1895. Millions of tales about deer and deer hunting have been generated since then, with thousands of new ones added each year, many of which have been told and retold countless times over the past century. Some of those tales will endure over the next 100 years and I think the ones in this book will be among them.

Despite claims to the contrary and complaints about the quality of the bucks produced in Michigan during recent years, all of the evidence indicates that more big racked bucks have been bagged by hunters in the state during the last 15 to 20 years than any other time over the past 100 years. Certainly some of the state's largest antlered bucks have been documented more recently. Detailed records maintained by Commemorative Bucks of Michigan (CBM), the state's big game record keeper, prove it. Let's hope that trend continues in the future.

You may have read one or more of the chapters in this book, or parts of them, before. They are all edited versions of magazine articles that were published over the years in Outdoor Life, North American Whitetail, Deer & Deer Hunting, Whitetail Strategies, Michigan Sportsman or Michigan Hunting & Fishing Magazines. Portions of the text were also included in Buck Fax, a quarterly magazine published by CBM, during the years I was editor of it, and three editions of Michigan Big Game Records, state record books that I authored/edited in cooperation with CBM. But this is the first time that such detailed coverage of so many of the state's biggest bucks has been presented in book form.

I thought it was about time. I hope you agree. If enough of you do, another book including different deer tales may be possible for the future.

Ray Caswell with Michigan's highest scoring 8-point rack scoring 175.
It's the only 8-pointer known taken in the state that qualifies for Boone and
Crockett Records. Caswell bagged the buck that grew the exceptional antlers
on November 17, 1978 in Delta County.

Chapter 1

One Of A Kind 8-Pointer

The odds of bagging a whitetail buck with 8-point antlers large enough to qualify for the Boone and Crockett (B&C) Record Book have got to be staggering, but whatever they are Ray Caswell from Escanaba surmounted them. There are a tremendous number of whitetail bucks with 8-point antlers shot in Michigan every fall, yet only one of those racks has ever been large enough to score more than 170, according to state records maintained by Commemorative Bucks of Michigan (CBM).

The antlers from the buck Caswell shot in Delta County score an even 175, making that rack the largest 8-pointer on record for the state. That head also holds the number one spot among typical gun kills in Delta County.

Ray had the record book rack for a number of years before he had it measured. He bagged the buck that was wearing them on November 17, 1978, which was the third day of the state's gun season, and it was no accident, although Lady Luck played a role in Caswell's discovery of the big buck. He was bear hunting during late September that year when the buck crossed a gravel road in front of a vehicle he was in about 9:00 a.m.

"I couldn't believe it when he ran across the road," Caswell said. "He was a dandy, boy. His antlers stuck way up in the air. I saw one or two other nice bucks that year, but their horns were nothing like those on this one.

"The day I saw him I stopped and checked his runway. He had that thing all tore up."

There was a lake across the road in the direction the buck was headed and the terrain was swampy , with tag alders bordering the road.

Ray never saw the buck again before hunting season, but every time he was in the area he checked the runway and usually found the buck's distinctive big tracks. It appeared as though the buck crossed the road often and had the trail "packed down like a cow path."

Ray was not only willing to forsake his normal stomping grounds to try for that buck, he said he "had to." Before gun season opened, he and one of his brothers, Wes, looked the runway over further and built blinds. A lot of big trees along the runway had been rubbed by the buck up to chest height, according to Caswell, and there were plenty of scrapes, too.

Ray placed his blind on the side of the road the buck had come from when he saw it. Wes picked a location on the opposite side of the road. On the side of the road Ray decided to hunt, the runway went through a stretch of alders then up over a hardwood ridge and back down into a swamp with mixed spruce, balsam and aspen trees. He put a blind on the ridge for optimum visibility a distance of 500 to 600 yards from the road. The blind was about 40 yards uphill from the deer trail at the base of a spruce tree.

On opening day of the 1978 deer gun season Ray sat in his blind waiting for the big buck with a single shot .45/70 rifle made by Harrington and Richardson. The rifle was mounted with a four power scope. Ray likes big bore rifles in single shot models, also owning a H&R .444.

Caswell hasn't always hunted with big bores though. In fact, the first whitetails he shot were dropped with small caliber rifles. His first buck, a 6-point, was shot with a caliber now illegal for deer hunting, the .22 rimfire. He shot the buck behind the shoulder, then got a couple of his brothers, who trailed the buck in the snow and finished it.

Ray said he was nine years old when he shot that first buck and he had shot one every fall since then during gun season through 1983 when I interviewed him. He was 28 years old at the time. Michigan has a law requiring youngsters to be 14 years old before they can hunt deer during gun season, but that law wasn't in effect back then, according to Caswell.

From the rimfire .22, Ray moved up to a .222 and took a number of deer with it, never losing an animal he hit. Caswell hunted with a shotgun and buckshot one year, killing a big 10-point buck at point blank range with a hip shot in a cedar swamp. The buck dressed out at 210 pounds and the antlers might have scored in the 160s. Those antlers were lost in a fire though, so we will never know what they scored.

Ray hunted deer with a .30-30 for a couple of years and a .32 before going to big bores. His preference for big carries over to muzzleloading rifles. He owned a .62 caliber front loader that he bagged at least one buck with, a 4-point.

The .45/70 was new in 1978. That was the first hunt Ray used it on and he was later glad he had it. Cartridges for the rifle look better suited for elephant or cape buffalo hunting than deer. The bullets weigh 405 grains, leaving the muzzle at 1,330 feet per second with 1,590 foot pounds of energy.

The first two days of the 1978 season were frustrating for both Ray and Wes. They didn't see a single whitetail, antlered or otherwise, during those two days. There were deer moving on the trail at night, according to tracks they saw, but the prints of the big one were absent.

Ray said there was too much traffic on the gravel road the first couple of days of the season, which curtailed deer activity on the trail crossing it. Worse yet, the trophy hunter started thinking that other hunters must have seen the buck cross the road before the season, as he had, and there was a distinct possibility someone else might have shot the whitetail he was after. With this in mind, Ray almost hunted somewhere else on the third day of the season. However, despite nagging doubts, he returned to his blind on the ridge where he had already spent two long, uneventful days and it's a good thing he did.

It was cold that morning. So cold that Ray remembers beginning to shake after only being seated for a matter of minutes. However, the hunter didn't have to withstand the cold for long. Ray had been in position for perhaps 20 minutes when he heard something big coming toward him along the trail from the spruce, balsam and aspen swamp. Whatever it was, it was making so much noise Caswell said he didn't think it could be the buck or any deer, for that matter.

It was the buck he saw two months earlier though. The antlered whitetail soon walked into view 40 yards away, unaware there was a hunter within miles. Ray cocked the hammer on his rifle at that point and the still air carried the metallic click to the buck's ears. The animal stopped at the sound, giving Ray an opportunity to aim and fire.

The buck immediately whirled back the way he had come from and was gone from sight in an instant. Ray listened to the huge whitetail crash his way through the swamp. Then the noise ended suddenly about 100 yards away. Ray thought the buck stopped there.

Instead of pushing the deer, Caswell decided to wait where he was. Then he heard something else coming. It proved to be his brother Wes. Wes heard the shot and wasted little time gong to check on Ray's success.

"Well, did you get 'im," were the first words out of Wes' mouth. Excitement was obvious in his voice.

"Ya, I poked him," was Ray's reply.

Before Ray could utter another word, Wes rattled off more questions and ended with, "Well, let's go get 'im," not giving Ray a chance to answer.

Wes was obviously anxious to get a close look at the buck. So was Ray, of course. He cautioned Wes that the buck might still be alive 100 yards away as they started on the whitetail's track. Fortunately, there was a light covering of snow on the ground, so tracking the buck wasn't difficult.

The whitetail wasn't waiting 100 yards ahead as Ray thought. The animal continued beyond that point, apparently not making enough noise for Ray to hear when it was that far away. Even more discouraging was the fact there was no blood whatsoever in that first 100 yards. However, the buck did start to bleed beyond that distance, and Ray said there was a lot of blood.

After trailing the buck 200 yards and still not finding him, Ray began getting concerned. Wes reassured him that the buck had to be dead with the amount of blood it was losing. Wes was right, but they had to go another 100 yards further before finding the fallen whitetail. Ray had climbed up on a knoll to look ahead and spotted his prize.

The buck was enormous. Ray said it was like field dressing a small cow. While removing the viscera the Caswells learned that the shot had been a good one after all, even though the buck had gone so far. The bullet had cut a major blood vessel above the heart and gone through the lungs, lodging in the opposite shoulder. The fact that the bullet didn't exit explains why there was no blood trail for the first 100 yards. The body cavity had to fill up with blood before it spilled out the entry wound.

The buck's size may have accounted for its stamina. Its heart was large enough to cover both of Ray's hands when held palms up next to each other. The buck was so heavy that Ray and Wes could not move it by themselves, even after the body cavity was emptied.

Wes went for help and got another brother to assist dragging the whitetail, and the three of them pulled the animal out to the road. They cut the buck's legs off at the knees to get it in Ray's vehicle. With the lower legs gone, the buck weighed 267 pounds. The animal easily weighed over 300 pounds on the hoof and proved to be five years old, according to Caswell.

Although Ray has taken other whitetail bucks that most hunters would rate as trophies, none compared with this one. He said that buck is definitely his most memorable kill. It's easy to understand why.

Two years after bagging the big buck Ray saw another enormous whitetail in the same area. This one crossed the same gravel road within 200 yards of where Ray first saw his record book buck. However, that buck wasn't using a runway and Ray didn't try for him. How did the antlers on that buck compare with those on the buck he got?

They were larger, according to Caswell. He said he made a quick count of the tines on one side before the buck went out of sight and he came up with eight. Ray figures that buck may have been a son of the whitetail he shot. He later heard about a big buck shot in the area by a woman, but wasn't sure who the hunter was or exactly how big the buck's antlers were. Maybe that rack will show up in the records in the future, if the antlers haven't already been measured. The county has produced its share of big antlered bucks that are already in state records.

During the fall of 1983, Ray and Wes were hunting for a potential book buck in Delta County that had 10 or 12-point antlers. Ray saw the buck once as the last rays of light were fading for the day, but there was a doe in front of the buck, preventing a clear shot, so he didn't shoot. Wes took a shot at the trophy buck another day through a small opening and missed.

Ray ended up filling his gun tag for 1983 with a decent 8-point buck. Not surprisingly, it was nothing like the one he bagged in 1978.

Ray's secret to success is really no secret at all. He simply tries to locate the territory of a big buck, either through an actual sighting or sign such as tracks, rubs and scrapes, then sets up an ambush. If he can't find a good location for a blind along a natural runway, he puts apples where he wants to sit, starting before the season opens. Local whitetails soon find the apples and begin feeding there.

What dimensions does an 8-point set of antlers have to possess to qualify for B&C? Well, just like any set of antlers, they should be wide, have long tines, heavy beams and be symmetrical. The rack worn by the buck Caswell shot certainly fits the bill.

The antlers have an inside spread of 20 6/8 inches. Beams are 25 3/8 and 26 2/8 inches long. Tines on the right side range between 10 2/8 and 13 6/8 inches in length. On the left they are 8 7/8 to 14 2/8 inches. The beams are 5 2/8 and 4 7/8 inches in circumference at the bases. And the rack is symmetrical. There are only 3 7/8 inches of deductions, which is the undoing of many sets of antlers that are potential book material.

There aren't too many sets of 8-point whitetail antlers that come with dimensions like those. The odds of getting a buck with antlers like that must be astronomical, considering how many 8s are shot every year. Congratulations to Ray Caswell for beating such long odds!

Bernie Murn with the head mount of 23-point nontypical he bagged in Keweenaw County during the 1980 gun season. The antlers measure 218 1/8 and are tied for fifth place among nontypicals in state records.

Chapter 2

Keweenaw County's Number One Nontypical

In many ways, Bernie Murn from Calumet is like many other whitetail hunters across Michigan who take buck hunting seriously. He spends a lot of time thinking about and preparing for the annual fall hunt. Deer hunting is also one of his favorite topics of conversation. And a week's vacation from work is always timed to coincide with the first week of gun deer season.

Once the season opens he works hard at deer hunting, with the ultimate goal of getting a crack at one of the big bucks he knows is out there. However, seeing deer, any deer, is still important. Murn doesn't have to hunt as hard as he does, but he wants to. He looks forward to that week more than any other one of the year, and he wants to take advantage of every minute of it possible.

The same things can probably be said of many other deer hunters. However, there are at least a couple of things about Bernie Murn and his deer hunting that aren't true for many other hunters. He's bagged a buck, for instance, wearing a nontypical rack large enough to qualify for listing in the Records of North American Big Game published by the Boone and Crockett Club. The antlers easily surpassed the minimum of 195, scoring 218 1/8 with one tine broken off.

In Michigan, the large set of antlers is tied for fifth place among nontypical gun kills in all time records, according to the 3rd edition of <u>Michigan Big Game Records</u> compiled by Commemorative Bucks of Michigan (CBM). The late Carl Mattson bagged a 21-pointer that scored the same in Iron County during the 1945 season. Mattson's buck was taken with a handgun and presently ranks as the highest scoring nontypical on record for the state in that category. The antlers of Murn's buck have 23 points.

At the time Bernie tagged his book buck (1980), it was ranked as the second largest on record for the state among nontypicals. Since then it has slowly gone down in rank as a few larger racks have been added to the records. However, the Murn head remains number one among nontypicals ever taken in Keweenaw County.

Quite a few bucks fell to Murn's rifle before he connected on the one with the exceptional rack. He guessed there were about 20 of them, including some with big racks, but nowhere near as big as the one he tagged during 1980. Although the antlers have been smaller, Bernie bagged at least one buck that had a bigger body than his book buck.

That animal had a trophy 10-point rack and weighed 230 pounds dressed. He guessed that the carcass of the Boone and Crockett (B&C) buck weighed about 200 pounds after field dressing. The skinned quarters weighed 172 pounds. Although Bernie didn't have the buck aged, he figures it was probably 5 1/2 years old.

Murn started deer hunting when he was about 15 years old and has been hunting ever since. The fall of 1993 marked his 42nd year of hunting whitetails. The success he has enjoyed over those years is amazing in view of the area he hunts. Most of his hunting has been done in Keweenaw County in the Upper Peninsula, which is the second thing that's different about him than most of the state's deer hunters. This is the northernmost county in Michigan and it has the dubious distinction of having the lowest deer density.

Winters are long in Keweenaw County with some of the greatest accumulations of snow recorded for the state, which makes living conditions tough for whitetails. The average annual snowfall in Keweenaw County is about 200 inches, according to the local National Weather Service office. However, for 1982, 260 inches of snow fell on the county. The total for 1981 was 315 inches and a whopping 355 inches for 1980.

Winter normally begins during November or December there and it's a rare year that snow doesn't remain on the ground into April. The county is at the tip of the Keweenaw Peninsula with Lake Superior on three sides. Its location in the big lake accounts for the abundance of snow that falls there.

As a whole, deer habitat in the county is marginal. It consists primarily of mature forests, but there are scattered openings remaining from old homesteads or logging operations. However, logging has been on the increase in the Keweenaw during recent years, which has improved habitat for deer in some areas. This country is rugged with plenty of lofty ridges high enough to be classified as mountains, plus swamps and few roads.

As a U.P. resident and avid deer hunter, I never gave Keweenaw County much consideration as having the potential of producing big bucks because of the habitat and severity of winters. The few antlers I saw from that county were small. The little information I had on deer there led me to incorrect conclusions. The Keweenaw is obviously a sleeper.

Bernie Murn opened my eyes as well as those of other hunters with his success in the county. Obviously, not all of the county's bucks have small racks. Even though deer are not abundant, some of the bucks born there live long enough to realize their full antler growth potential. The fact that there is normally only three to four hunters per square mile in the county, helps make that possible. In remote terrain that is hard to get to, there's probably little or no hunting pressure.

When you put few deer together with few hunters in a county like Keweenaw I would expect a low rate of success. However, the success ratio for the county is anything but low, according to former DNR District Wildlife Biologist El Harger. Harger is retired, but the county was in his district during the period when Murn got his B&C buck.

"Deer hunting success is up there around 46 percent in Keweenaw County," Harger said.

As amazing as it may seem, that means hunters who try their luck in an area with the lowest deer density in the state are among the most successful in the state. However, most of the deer hunters who try their luck there are probably locals who are familiar with the country. The closest any other county in Michigan comes to the success in Keweenaw is Menominee where there are many more deer, with a 35 percent success ratio. Most counties with more deer have a rate of success that is less than 20 percent. Of course, those counties have many more hunters, too.

Harger said the number of deer in the county ranges from five to 10 per square mile, but is probably closer to the lower figure. He confirmed that the county produces its share of trophy bucks.

"Trophy hunting is the only real plus for the county because there are not a lot of deer," Harger said. "For the hunter intent on looking for a trophy, that's the place to go. The Keweenaw is one of the areas I recommend for strictly trophy hunting."

21

But how do those bucks live so long and grow trophy racks with all that snow to contend with? A tough winter definitely puts stress on bucks, and those that survive in a weakened condition aren't going to produce racks as big as healthy bucks.

"Once bucks make it through a couple of winters, they aren't as affected by the weather," was Harger's reply. He said that by then they've grown large enough to reach food that may not be accessible to the average deer, plus they've learned where to find food and shelter when the snow gets deep.

Although deer numbers are not high anywhere in Keweenaw County, there are a couple of locations where deer numbers are greater than elsewhere in the county. One such location is south and west of Schlatter Lake at the extreme eastern tip of the county. The second area lies between the communities of Gay and Betsy on the southeast side of the county.

It should be apparent by now that the area Murn hunts is as unique as the big-racked buck he bagged there. He likes the country and that's why he continues to hunt it. He also likes the solitude that is possible in hunting an area with few deer. Bernie said he may see one or two other hunters during the first couple of days of the season, but after that it is unusual to encounter anyone else.

Due to the low number of deer in the county, hunters such as Murn who are consistently successful must have a good working knowledge of the terrain and where whitetails normally are within it. Bernie spends a lot of time in the woods both before and after deer season during which he is always looking for deer sign. He combines scouting for deer with grouse hunting and fishing before deer season opens and rabbit hunting afterward.

While the location of any deer sign is logged in his memory, what he especially takes note of are big tracks and big trees that have been rubbed by a trophy buck's antlers. Bernie said big tracks are most often made by big bucks where he hunts, but not always. Sometimes an old doe will leave big prints. However, there's no mistaking what type of deer is responsible for big rubs. Only mature bucks with wide antlers are capable of rubbing full-fledged trees.

Once Murn locates the haunt of a big buck, he returns as often as possible in an effort to learn more about the animal.

"Those big guys have set patterns," he said.

He tries to find out what that pattern of movement is without spooking the animal. Bernie said big bucks change their habits, at least for a while, if they are disturbed. Bucks in Keweenaw County simply don't encounter many people at any time of the year.

When hunting for a big buck, Bernie usually alternates between sitting and stillhunting. If he thinks the deer will be moving, he sits. If he thinks a buck is laid up somewhere, he moves. On days when the right snow conditions exist, when it is quiet underfoot, he may do some tracking.

Antler rubs on exceptionally large trees are what clued Bernie in on the presence of the B&C buck he bagged during the 1980 season. The whitetail lived in a location that was extremely thick. The spot had been logged a number of years before and an abundance of saplings sprouted there producing almost a solid wall of young trees. There was a series of small swamps below the cutover area and big ridges above.

The situation was ideal for harboring a big buck. If the animal was forced out of the thick cover provided by the saplings, he could go downhill into a swamp, which would also provide plenty of cover, or uphill on one of the ridges where a buck could easily outdistance a hunter. Bernie commented that locations like that one are so attractive to big bucks that when a dominant buck is removed, another one soon takes its place. And the new buck's pattern of movement, which is often dictated by the terrain, will be similar to that of the buck that was bagged. Bernie has tagged other bucks in the same area since 1980.

Murn jumped the book buck one day while hunting. Although he didn't get a look at the animal, he knew it had a big rack. He heard the antlers rattling against saplings as the buck ran off. Just about seven full days of the season elapsed before Bernie finally got a look at the buck. He was sitting at the time. His stand was in the vicinity of some of the buck's rubs and scrapes. There was a trace of snow on the ground.

The big buck hunter heard the animal coming long before he saw it. He looked at his watch when he first heard the whitetail. It was 20 minutes after four in the afternoon. The buck took a step or two and stopped, then moved a few more steps ahead after a pause. Each step was bringing the buck closer to Murn, but the animal was exhibiting extreme caution, which is not unusual for mature whitetails.

Nonetheless, the buck's pace resulted in the buildup of tension in the hunter through anticipation of a shot, although at the same time, he wasn't sure if the animal that was approaching was a buck or doe. Bernie hoped it was a buck, but not just any buck - the big one.

The thickness of the cover was adding to the tension. The deer was taking forever to step into view. There was the possibility that before that happened the whitetail could change directions or simply pass by unseen behind a screen of saplings. The heavy brush might also prevent a clear shot even though parts of the animal might be visible.

You know what it's like. The wait for a deer to appear once the animal's foot steps are heard can be pure agony, especially if it takes a long time.

After a full 20, nerve-racking minutes the deer finally walked into Murn's field of view. He saw the deer was a buck at that point and that it was a big animal. The cover was so thick though that Bernie only saw a portion of the buck's rack, not enough to tell its full dimensions, and he had to hold his fire because there was just not an opening big enough to insure passage of a 180 grain bullet from his .300 Savage.

The buck eventually walked into what looked like a small opening in the brush and Bernie was ready, sending a bullet toward its shoulder. The shot connected, but still clipped two or three bits of brush before striking the buck. That's an indication of how thick the cover was in the buck's core area.

Even though Bernie scored a good hit, the buck ran a short distance before dropping. The hunter got his first good look at the buck's massive antlers as he approached the fallen animal and he was amazed at their size. He had no idea the rack was that big.

Despite the fact the antlers were big, Murn never dreamed they were big enough to qualify for B&C listing. Although he is a big buck hunter, he readily admits bagging a book buck was the furthest thing from his mind. Bernie knew a record book for listing exceptional whitetail antlers existed, but that's about it.

Meanwhile, the buck's cape and antlers were given to a taxidermist for mounting. The work still hadn't been done after a year, so Bernie transferred them to another, more dependable taxidermist, Pat Scott at Merriman. The antlers were finally measured for B&C consideration while in Scott's hands. It was 1982 by that time.

Despite his good fortune in bagging a buck with such impressive antlers, Bernie Murn doesn't figure he's any different than many other buck hunters across Michigan. In many ways, he's not. However, the book buck he bagged and the area he hunts sets him apart from most other deer hunters.

Murn's secrets for success on land with few deer are actually no secrets at all. He spends as much time as possible scouting, and once the season opens, he hunts hard. The only advice he has for other hunters follows along the same lines. He recommends "doing a lot of scouting" and "working hard" at deer hunting.

Dave Wellman of Bark River displays the head mount of a 21-point nontypical taken by the late Carl Mattson in Iron County during 1945. The antlers score the same as Murn's Monster.

Craig Calderone displays Michigan's highest scoring typical buck, with measurements totaling 193 2/8. The buck that grew the tremendous rack fell to an arrow launched from Calderone's bow on November 6, 1986, his 27th birthday. The buck is not listed in state records, but can be found in records maintained by the Boone and Crockett and Pope and Young Clubs.

Chapter 3

Birthday Buck

The years 1984 through 1986 are extremely important in Michigan's big buck hunting history. State record bucks were bagged each of those years. Mark Ritchie started off the three-year streak with a 10-pointer scoring 186 1/8, the highest scoring typical buck on record for the state up until that time.

Mitch Rompola added a state record bow kill in 1985, a 12-pointer scoring 181 7/8. Then, in 1986, Craig Calderone from Jackson set new marks for both typical bow and alltime kills. The typical 14-pointer he claimed with bow and arrow on November 6th that year set two new records. The rack is the only typical on record for the state with a net score that exceeds 190, scoring 193 2/8.

Oddly enough, both of the highest scoring typicals bagged by bowhunters in Michigan were tagged on the archers' birthdays. Rompola scored on his 37th birthday and details about how he accomplished it are included in another chapter. Calderone connected on his 27th birthday. What outstanding birthday presents those whitetails were!

Shooting a state record buck was the furthest thing from Craig's mind during the fall of 1986. However, after talking with him, it was obvious he deserved to take such a fine specimen. He earned the chance that he capitalized on.

Craig is a dedicated bowhunter, having started when he was 14 years old. He got his first bow and arrows from his brother Mike. Craig finds the challenge of trying for a mature buck with bow and arrow personally rewarding, regardless of the outcome. He has a high level of respect for whitetail deer and especially adult bucks. His words

Mark Ritchie with 10-point typical scoring 186 1/8 that he collected during 1984. (Photo courtesy Ken Sharpe)

adequately express his philosophy.

"To me, it's sad to shoot any deer," Calderone said, "but it's a challenge getting a big buck. There's no satisfaction for me in shooting a small deer. I love just getting out in the woods where it's quiet. I enjoy scouting the most."

And Craig does a lot of scouting, year-round, as much to be among whitetails; watching them, admiring them and learning about them, as preparing for hunting season. He spends a lot of time on high ridges and along fence rows with a 30 power spotting scope watching deer. Calderone admits a set of binoculars would suffice for much of this type of scouting, but he really likes to zoom in to see what he's looking at.

During the 13 years Calderone had been bowhunting for deer through 1986, he had tagged 11 of them. Some of those whitetails have been bucks with good racks. The antlers from two bucks he bagged meet the Pope and Young minimum for typical racks, which is 125. Interestingly, both of those bucks were also bagged on November 6th.

In 1982 Craig arrowed an 8-point that measured between 129 and 130. A 9-point he dropped during 1983 scored around 131. Calderone also claimed an 11-point buck during 1984 and 9-point in 1985. The rack buck he bow-bagged during 1985 was taken on opening day of gun season.

Craig said he hadn't hunted deer with a gun since 1980.

Bowhunting for whitetails is legal during firearm season in Michigan as long as the hunter has a gun deer license in possession and wears orange, as required by law.

Once hunting season opens, Calderone spends as much time as he can in the field, continuing routine scouting as well as hunting. He doesn't report for work until 11:00 a.m., so he hunts every morning of the week. Besides morning hunting, he hunts an average of three evenings a week.

Early in the fall, before the rut starts, Craig selects stand sites near trails leading to and from bedding and feeding areas. However, he tries to get off of main trails and in thick cover. He's learned that these are the areas where the chances of getting a shot at a dominant buck are highest. If possible, Craig said he likes to set up in a location where there's thick cover, yet he can see a distance from his tree stand so he can keep tabs on the movement of deer around him.

Once the rut starts and scrapes begin appearing, Calderone often watches active scrapes, and that's how he got the state record whitetail.

Craig reports having fewer chances at bucks during the fall of 1986 than 1985. He routinely passes up shots at bucks with small racks, adding to his knowledge about whitetails by watching them. There were five bucks that he passed up during 1986, with antlers ranging from forks to small 8-points. All of those bucks were probably yearlings or 1 1/2 years old.

Spike bucks are rare in Jackson County where Craig hunts. The county is in the southern part of the state where winters are mild and preferred deer foods are abundant, resulting in excellent antler growth among bucks. Most yearling bucks grow 6-point antlers for their first set in that part of the state, but some sprout forks and others 8s.

Jackson County is among the top producers of bucks with big racks in the southern part of the state, according to Commemorative Bucks of Michigan (CBM) records. Through 1993 there were six Boone and Crockett (B&C) bucks, two of which are nontypicals, from the county listed in CBM records. That number excludes Calderone's buck. The county's largest typical recorded in state records is an 11-pointer scoring 179 4/8 that was shot with a shotgun during 1980 by John Cubic. More on this at the end of the chapter.

The county's best nontypical was taken by Steve Crocker during 1989 with a shotgun. The 18-pointer scores 201 1/8. Bowhunters are well represented in the records from Jackson County, accounting for a significant number of entries, including two of the B&C typicals taken in 1990 and '91, one of which is covered in another chapter in this book. The highest scoring nontypical bow kill on record for the state came from the county during 1993.

Besides passing up more bucks during 1985 than a year later, Calderone also let some big bucks go by before taking the 9-point he

Mitch Rompola with 12-point bow kill from 1985 that measured 181 7/8.

tagged. In fact, a couple of the bucks he passed up that year may have had better racks than the one he took. It was soon after daylight on November 15th when Craig arrowed the 9-point. He counted five points on one beam before taking the shot and thought there were as many on the opposite side, but there only proved to be four. A couple of the bucks he passed up earlier that fall may have been 10-pointers.

When bowhunting during gun season, as he was when taking the 9-point, Craig usually tries to ambush bucks along escape routes where he thinks other hunters will push deer. That strategy resulted in his success during 1985.

In 1986 Calderone missed a shot at a 10-point buck before connecting on the record whitetail. He got the shot after stalking the animal rather than while waiting in ambush for the deer to come to him. It was late October when he spotted the buck in the company of a doe and the pair stayed together. There's a good chance the doe was in heat. At any rate, Craig snuck within 30 yards of the buck when it bolted and that's when he shot.

The state record holder said he seldom takes a bow shot that far away, but did in that case due to the circumstances. When stand hunting, most of the shots he gets are under 20 yards because of the thick cover he's hunting. If a chance for a long shot comes up when stand hunting,

Craig usually waits rather than risk a miss or wounding a whitetail.

His reluctance to take long shots is not due to lack of competency with bow and arrow, but more out of respect for the animals. He also has a lot of patience, an important virtue for big buck hunters. By waiting, the odds of an assured clean kill often improve.

Calderone had been hunting with a PSE Citation bow set at 75 pounds. He spends a lot of time shooting it; every day during summer and winter, so he's confident of connecting when he does take a shot. His choice of broadheads are Rothaar Snuffers.

Craig thinks he saw the record book buck he bagged during 1986 on two occasions before the day he shot it. He was scouting both times their paths crossed. The first time was the third week of October. He jumped a group of three bucks at a distance of 200 yards.

The Jackson resident got his binoculars up fast enough to get a good look at the first buck in the group and he saw it had a big rack. He didn't get a very good look at the second buck, but was able to glass the third one and it had a rack with about a 16-inch spread. Craig later found out that the number two buck's antlers were second in size among the three animals, with a 20-inch spread. That buck was shot during gun season by another hunter.

On November 1st the bowhunter looked over the area where he jumped the three bucks and found an active scrape. He also got another glimpse of a big buck that day, the one he probably got. The animal was about 75 yards away in thick brush, so he didn't get a good look at it.

Calderone was perched in a tree stand within view of that scrape on the morning of November 6, 1986. He had to climb 25 feet to reach the stand. He wanted to be high to reduce the chances of being detected by any deer that came along. It was a cold, crisp morning with frost on the ground and a temperature of 28 degrees.

Daylight came at about 7:00 a.m. that day. A doe passed by about that time. Approximately 15 minutes later, Craig was treated to an awe-inspiring sight he'll probably never forget as a buck with a huge rack jumped a fence 65 yards away and came toward the scrape he was watching. The whitetail went around a big deadfall when approaching the scrape, and after clearing the obstruction at a distance of 18 yards, Calderone released what would become the most important arrow of his hunting career.

The shaft was well placed, but only pierced one lung due to the angle of the shot. Craig found the once-in-a-lifetime buck at the end of a sparse, 200-yard blood trail. Antler beams carried 14 points, eight on the right side and six on the left. The longest tine was 11 inches in length and the inside spread was close to 23 inches.

The fact that he might have tagged a state record buck didn't occur to Calderone at the time he scored. He was overwhelmed enough by the realization that the antlers were likely large enough to meet the

B&C minimum. After Craig got the buck home, he and his brother Mike measured the rack, and it was at that point that the true proportions of the antlers began to sink in, but it sunk in slowly. The rack was measured and remeasured, not believing the true score was actually over the 190 mark.

It was true though. After the 60-day drying period was up, Craig took the antlers to B&C measurer Bob Jones from Portland. He came up with a score of 193 2/8. The gross score was 206 3/8 and there were 13 1/8 inches of deductions. The final tally would have obviously been higher had the rack been more symmetrical. One tine that was broken reduced the score by about two inches. There was also a sticker point over an inch long below the brow tine on the right antler.

Inside spread of the antlers was 22 2/8 inches. The left beam was 27 7/8 inches long and the right beam was 28 3/8 inches in length. Craig Calderone has every reason to be a proud bowhunter. He had accomplished every archer's dream. More importantly, taking that whitetail was a dream come true for him. The buck had a dressed weight of 199.5 pounds and was 4 1/2 years old.

However, the story behind Calderone's record buck does not yet have a totally happy ending. Unfortunately, there have been times when Craig admitted that he wished he hadn't bagged the great buck. The head is not officially recognized as a state record by CBM and, as a result, a listing for it can't be found in any of the state record books produced by CBM. But the antlers do have a place in national records maintained by the Pope and Young and Boone and Crockett Clubs.

Why the difference? Calderone's record setting buck was initially listed in state records, but was removed in 1988 due to a couple of tickets Craig received for game law violations that had nothing to do with the buck. CBM bylaws prevent the listing of a hunter for a period of three to five years, depending on the offense.

Both of the tickets Calderone received were for illegal shining of deer. The first offense was when he was in college and there was a rifle in the vehicle. The second offense was after he got his big buck and a new law went into effect prohibiting shining deer during November. Calderone did not have a weapon with him when ticketed the second time.

For more details about the controversy surrounding Calderone's buck, refer to the 2nd edition of Michigan Big Game Records. A chapter in the 256-page book thoroughly discusses the issue. Instructions for ordering that book and others can be found elsewhere in this book.

The 5-year probationary period provided for in CBM's bylaws has expired and the Calderone head is once again eligible for entry in state records. I hope Craig takes advantage of the opportunity to re-enter the whitetail and the entry is accepted. The buck and the bowhunter both deserve a special place in Michigan's deer hunting history.

Close up of the mount of Craig Calderone's impressive Michigan typical.

Mark Ritchie with the highest scoring typical presently listed in state records. Measurements totaled 186 1/8.

Chapter 4

Washtenaw Wallhanger

Mark Ritchie from Dexter wanted to bag a buck with a nice 8 or 10-point rack suitable for mounting during most of his first 15 years of deer hunting. He finally got a buck with a head suitable for hanging on a wall during the fall of 1984 and now he's the envy of many Michigan deer hunters.

The typical rack from the buck Ritchie bagged wasn't just big. It's the biggest listed in state records maintained by Commemorative Bucks of Michigan (CBM), outscoring the previous record typical by 4 4/8 inches. Mark's 10-point rack scored 186 1/8. A head from a buck bagged by the late Lester Bowen in Ionia County during 1947 was the previous state record. Those antlers measured 181 2/8.

Oddly enough, the record deer Bowen shot is the only whitetail he collected during his hunting career. That can't be said for Ritchie, who was 29 at the time he took his record buck. Mark tagged deer 13 out of the 15 years he had hunted them through 1984. All but one of those whitetails were bucks. Each of those kills was made in Washtenaw County within a five square mile area.

Mark's first deer was a doe, the only female whitetail he had shot before collecting the record animal. That doe may have been a record of sorts, too. The young hunter was 14 years old at the time, the first year he could legally hunt deer with a gun in Michigan. His father had to work on opening day of the season, so he talked his mother into taking him hunting that evening.

Mark took a stand in an old sheep loading ramp overlooking an apple orchard and collected the doe with a slug from a 12 gauge shotgun when she came in to feed. The downed doe was so big, Mrs. Ritchie had to ask a friend to help them move the deer. When the field dressed doe was weighed, she tipped the scales at 240 pounds, which is certainly among the top weights recorded for whitetail does, if not the heaviest. Upon checking several normally reliable reference books on deer, there were no record weights for does listed as opposed to numerous listings of big-bodied bucks.

Although the big buck Mark bagged during November of 1984 was his first that made the record books, he came close on two other occasions. He didn't connect during those occasions, but after seeing how his record rack scored, he was convinced the other two bucks wore antlers that would have measured up to Boone and Crockett (B&C) standards. A minimum score of 170 is required for typical antlers to qualify for B&C listing. Mark said the first book buck that got away had antlers at least as big as the one he got and may have been bigger.

In fact, he thought there was a chance the buck bagged during 1984 was the same one that eluded him a number of years earlier. Both whitetails were seen in the same area. He had the book buck aged to find out. It was only 4 1/2 years old, not old enough to have been the same deer.

It was opening morning of gun season at 8:00 a.m. when Ritchie saw the first book buck that got away. A doe appeared first and she was soon followed by the enormous whitetail. The big buck was about 100 yards away when he first saw it and it was coming toward him, so he waited, expecting to get a much closer shot.

The deer disappeared behind a thorn tree and never reappeared. After 15 minutes elapsed and the doe was long since gone, Mark figured the buck had to have laid down under the tree because he could see all around it. Filled with excitement and anticipation, Mark slowly crept toward the tree with his shotgun ready. What happened to the buck was apparent when he reached the tree without seeing the deer.

There was a ditch that was about four feet deep directly behind the tree, which Ritchie didn't know existed. The buck stepped into it, vanishing from sight. To add insult to injury, the antlered whitetail followed the ditch around Mark, coming within 30 yards of him, and rejoined the doe once past the hunter. Mark is convinced the buck had to crouch down and sneak by him in the ditch to go unseen.

"From that day on I was kicking myself for not taking a shot at that buck when I first saw it at 100 yards, but I wanted a closer shot," Mark admitted. "That deer was a monster 10 or 12-pointer. When I first saw it I thought it was an elk. It gave me that kind of impression. It was as big as my record buck or maybe even bigger."

Another potential book buck that Ritchie never fired a shot at was also saved by uneven terrain. It was the fourth day of the state's 15-day gun season and he was on his way to a stand at the time, which was about 4:00 p.m. Mark said he was walking along the edge of a woods, which was on his left, and a plowed field was on his right. He was examining numerous deer tracks in bare soil along the edge of the plowed field when he looked up to discover a "monstrous" white-racked buck was walking parallel to him in the open field, unaware of his presence.

The distance between hunter and deer was estimated at 70 yards. Mark dropped to a kneeling position to steady himself for a shot. Then he decided to go to a prone position, but waited to shoot, thinking the buck was headed for a piece of woods directly in front of him and a better shot would be offered.

All of a sudden, the buck's legs started getting shorter, and in seconds the whitetail was gone. Although the ground in the field looked level, it wasn't. When Mark investigated, he discovered that the buck had been walking along the top of a hill and simply walked off of it away from him when it disappeared.

That same buck was bagged by another hunter two days later, according to Ritchie. The rack carried 14 points. Those antlers hadn't been measured by the time Mark got his booner, but he was confident they would qualify for B&C listing.

Big racked bucks aren't unusual in the area Ritchie hunts, which is private property he has permission to use, although they are by no means common either. Besides the three bruisers Mark has had contact with, another 14-point buck that was supposed to have a gigantic rack was hit by a car and killed. And there was still at least one trophy left that Mark knew of.

The day after Mark tagged his record buck, acquaintances of his saw a tremendous buck in the headlights of their car as it crossed a road ahead of them about 11:00 p.m.

"They said it had points everywhere," Mark stated. "The way they described it, it sounded like a big nontypical."

The buck Mark's friends saw might have been a nontypical 17-pointer that Darryl Carr from Dexter bagged with his car in Washtenaw County on October 29th, 1986. He said it was about 8:00 p.m. that night when he hit the big buck. He was driving up a hill at the time and the lights from an oncoming pickup truck partially blinded him. The buck jumped across the front of the truck, landing in front of Carr's car. The vehicle sustained $4,500 damage from impact with the deer, which had a dressed weight of 236 pounds. The antlers had a B&C score of 209 1/8.

The book buck Ritchie eventually got was seen crossing in the exact same place as the nontypical during late September or early October of 1984. It was 3:00 p.m. and the big animal was accompanied by another "respectable" buck. The two bucks were observed sparring in a field nearby at a later date.

Ritchie knew the exceptional buck was around as a result of these sightings that were related to him. He started hunting the area with bow and arrow during October, but never saw the big boy. However, he did find a couple of scrapes side-by-side that he felt were made by the buck.

Mark was nestled in a hollowed out brushpile overlooking those scrapes on the second day of gun season. The first day had been uneventful without a single deer sighting. Most of the second day was the same, but what happened about 4:30 p.m. made the wait worthwhile. The once-in-a-lifetime buck appeared, trailing a doe by about 30 yards.

"I couldn't believe it when I saw him coming," Mark said. "He used his horns just like a person would use their hands to move brush out of the way, as he came through the woods."

The pair of deer was moving painstakingly slow. They were nervous, having approached from the direction where another hunter disappeared minutes before, and they were downwind from Mark's position. The animals appeared as though they knew something was wrong, but hadn't pinpointed danger.

Ritchie said he uses fox urine to help cover his scent and that might have helped to confuse the buck and doe. The doe was edgier than her escort. She kept prancing back and forth. Mark had a single shot shotgun, so he knew he only had one chance to connect and he didn't want to gamble on trying to rush his one and only shot.

Mark had purchased the used gun at a garage sale the previous summer. He bought it for $70 because he said it looked like the perfect deer gun. It was an Ithaca with a Deer Slayer barrel, a scope and sling.

"Even though I owned a 12 gauge Remington model 1100, I felt more confident with that single shot. The minute I got it home I set up a concrete block at 100 yards to see how it shot. I pulled the trigger and the block disintegrated. It was right on.

"About every deer I've gotten has been with one shot. The first shot has gotta count."

Mark prefers Brenneke slugs and that was what he was using when he got his record buck. The buck was 60 yards away when the hunter first saw its rack. It closed the distance to 30 yards over a span of 10 minutes before it was in position for a shot he was satisfied with.

"When I finally made my shot," Mark said, "I had to settle for the neck because he parked his front section right in front of a tree that was a foot in diameter and hung his big neck out looking around the tree right towards me."

His 12 gauge Ithaca mounted with a quick point Weaver scope was already at his shoulder. Ritchie put the scope's red dot on the buck's neck and gently squeezed the gun's trigger. The shot was the best he had ever made on a whitetail up until that time, dropping the animal instantly with a broken neck.

Ken Sharpe, a hunting buddy of Mark's, was on stand 60 yards away when Ritchie connected. He joined his partner soon after the shot and said Mark was as excited as "a 14-year-old kid with his first deer." Although that was Mark's first sighting of the record buck, Ken saw it twice within 20 minutes that morning, both times from his vehicle.

Ken said he and his father hunted together for a couple of hours that morning. They were on their way home at 9:00 a.m. when they spotted the big buck chasing does 40 yards from the road in a cow posture. They had no access to the private land, so there was no opportunity to try for the deer. They watched the buck run off out of sight, then heard three or four shots in that direction.

They had every reason to believe the buck might have been shot - until 20 minutes later. Ken was picking up another hunter a quarter-of-a-mile from where he originally saw the book buck when he saw it again. The deer went into a five-acre patch of woods where Sharpe thought it would remain the rest of the day. His hunch proved correct.

Mark said his record deer had a dressed weight of 208 pounds a week after it was tagged. The antlers originally had an inside spread of 19 1/2 inches, which was down to 19 inches after the 60-day drying period required before antlers can be measured for record book consideration. The longest tines were 11 3/4 inches in length. The tips of each beam came close to touching, with only 3 1/2 inches separating them.

The narrow gap between beam tips might explain why Mark never found any antler rubs on big trees in the buck's territory. The tips were too close together for the buck to rub on anything but small trees.

Mitch Rompola of Traverse City with his best Michigan buck so far, a 12-pointer scoring 181 7/8, taken on his 37th birthday.

Chapter 5

Book Buck Bowhunter

November 8, 1985 was a big day for Mitch Rompola of Traverse City. It was his birthday, his 37th, but there was something extra special about this one. That's the day he bow-bagged a buck wearing a new state record typical rack.

With a score of 181 7/8, the antlers rank number 4 in the state among typicals taken by any means, according to CBM records, and at the top of the list for bow kills. Mitch was the second bowhunter in the state to bag a buck with antlers exceeding a score of 170, the minimum required for a entry in Boone and Crockett Records. Robert Savola was the first with an Alger County 10-pointer scoring 170 7/8 in 1981. While luck played a major role in Savola's success, the opposite is true for Mitch.

Rompola's record book buck was by no means a fluke for him. He knew the buck was there and hunted specifically for him. The booner is Mitch's biggest-racked buck from Michigan, but far from the only trophy whitetail he's anchored with an arrow in the state. Five other bucks had fallen as a result of his bowhunting expertise before the record animal that have antlers qualifying for Pope and Young and CBM listing. Since then he's taken plenty of others that fit in the same category. His next best buck has a score of 161 and ranks 26th in the state among typical bow kills, according to the 3rd edition of <u>Michigan Big Game Records.</u>

Put simply, an intimate knowledge of the area and deer he's hunting, are largely responsible for Mitch's enviable record. Armed with this knowledge, Rompola has been able to best determine where and when the bucks he's after are most vulnerable. He also has the discipline to pass up chancy shots and persistence to continue hunting until he gets the shot he wants, even if it means hunting with a bow during gun season.

Intensive, fulltime scouting is the key to Mitch's success. He keeps tabs on deer by interpreting their sign (tracks, trails, beds, rubs and scrapes), locating preferred foods and actual sightings of animals. He's also intimately familiar with the area he hunts in, having thoroughly mapped six square miles of it to show how deer utilize that habitat.

Mitch obviously devotes more time to deer hunting than most hunters do, but that's what it takes to be consistently successful on book bucks. He studies whitetails year round.

"When most hunters have quit thinking about deer hunting at the end of the season, I will be preparing for the next season," Rompola said. "By the time the hunting season arrives, I will have put in more time preparing for it than most hunters will spend hunting. By the end of the season, I will have used over 40 different stand sites. I have taken my hunting to such an extreme level that it would boggle the minds of most hunters."

"For over 30 years I have kept a hunting journal on my studies and observations. Data from the past 10 years (1980 through 1990) shows that if I could have taken every big buck I had in bow range, I would have over 50 in the records. From the last 10 years I have seen 68 big bucks, 56 of which were in bow range. I managed to take 10 of those."

Rompola has found that knowing the habits and home ranges of family groups of does and fawns could be just as important a part of successful big buck hunting as isolating information about bucks themselves. The reason for this is no matter how unpredictable or elusive bucks are during most of the fall, once the rut begins they can be found mingling with does and fawns. Of course, Mitch does his best to keep tabs on bucks he's interested in, in addition to does and fawns, while scouting. The more he learned about the area he hunts and the local deer herd, the easier it became to pattern the movements of both bucks and does.

Other hunting pressure was fit into Rompola's formula for book buck success, too. Bucks simply don't live long where hunting pressure is heavy. To grow record book racks, bucks have to survive two or three seasons, and bucks are most likely to accomplish this where there is little or no hunting pressure.

Mitch found a hot spot for trophy bucks close to home through his scouting efforts. It is a large swamp that few other hunters penetrate because it is thick and wet. The swamp has a fairly high resident population of does and fawns that attract bucks from surrounding areas during the rut, and there are some bucks that live in the swamp most of the year, too. Pressure from other hunters around the perimeter of the swamp also increases the number of bucks inhabiting its interior during hunting seasons.

The number of bucks is highest in Rompola's hot spot during mid to late November, when Michigan's gun deer season is open. That's when deer hunting pressure is heaviest and the rut is still on. Three of Mitch's six Michigan book bucks taken through 1985 were arrowed after November 15th. In fact, they were bagged during consecutive years, 1982-84. It is legal to bowhunt for deer during the firearms hunt as long as the hunter has a valid gun deer license and wears at least an orange hat, as required by law.

In 1982 Mitch scored on November 22nd. The buck he bagged that day had the best typical rack to his credit until 1985. He saw the buck a number of times before finally connecting and he thought its rack might be large enough to meet the B&C minimum of 170.

"I saw him cut through the same place three times within a week," Rompola recalled, "and another 8-point buck was always with him. I went in there one evening and sat in an old windfall near where I had been seeing them. It was about 5:20 p.m. when I heard deer coming. They were cracking brush and splashing water.

"The big buck was in the front and he stopped right where I wanted him to, 18 steps away. I couldn't have asked for anything better. I drew back and he looked right at me. He was starting to run when I released."

Mitch's arrow was too fast for the buck though. As soon as the shaft connected, the trophy hunter dropped his bow and ran into the open to better see where the arrowed buck went. After the big buck was gone, Mitch turned around to find the 8-pointer staring at him. He went through the motions of drawing and releasing an imaginary bow and arrow as the smaller buck stood there.

As it turned out, the big buck's 10-point antlers fell short of the B&C minimum by nine inches, scoring 161. That buck was 6 1/2 years old and had a dressed weight of 238 pounds.

The vast majority of Rompola's bucks have been shot from ground blinds rather than tree stands. The main reason for this is there simply hasn't been any trees, or trees suitable for placing platforms in, where he does most of his hunting. A lot of trees in the swamp where Mitch hunts have been blown down during storms and he frequently uses these windfalls as ground blinds. However, a hollow stump served as his blind when he scored during 1984.

Because the area Mitch hunts is so thick, he clears trails that enable him to reach stands without making noise, which is essential to minimize disturbance of deer and reduce the chances of them detecting his presence. These trails are usually cleared during winter months. On days when conditions are such that even an approach on one of his trails would be noisy, he doesn't hunt.

When approaching spots where he will post, Mitch moves into or across the wind to prevent his scent from alerting whitetails. His approach does not take him across trails he expects bucks to use either. He never uses cover or sex scents in his deer hunting. Mitch doesn't feel they are necessary if hunters approach stands properly and stands are positioned with wind direction and deer movements in mind.

When ever possible, Rompola selects stands to intercept book bucks near their bedding areas, either as they leave them in the evening or when returning to them in the morning. He locates bedding areas by looking for a concentration of rubs and scrapes with a patch of thick, almost impenetrable (to hunters), cover nearby. Bucks will bed in thickets and because they spend most of their days there, rubs and scrapes will be numerous in the vicinity. Mitch said bucks frequently bed on small patches of dry ground surrounded by water in the swamp where he has had his best success.

In some cases, the stands he selects to wait out bucks put him in a position to see the animals, but not close enough for the shot he wants. Under those circumstances, he is then able to adjust his position appropriately for another day. Mitch's hunt for the whitetail that proved to be a state record began during November of 1984 as soon as his tag went on a 15-pointer scoring 146 7/8. The two bucks were only bedding about 100 yards apart and he saw the record animal a couple of times before scoring on the 15-point.

One of the main differences between the buck Mitch got in 1984 and the other book animals to his credit is he missed a shot at it, but he kept hunting for it, hoping he would get another chance at the trophy whitetail and he finally did. It was November 14th when Rompola missed the deer and it was 11 days later before he got another crack at the buck. As mentioned earlier, a hollow stump was selected as a blind that year.

Mitch was standing in the stump on the 14th when his intended target appeared. It took the whitetail 20 minutes to get into position for a shot at a distance of 13 steps, from the time the bowhunter first saw it. When the buck was in perfect position, he turned his head away from Rompola and started licking himself. Mitch said he almost felt sorry for the buck as he calmly drew and released, then couldn't believe it when the arrow went high.

The experienced archer got a late start on November 25th and hadn't reached his stump blind yet when he saw the same buck coming his way. Mitch crawled up to a point behind the stump and got ready to shoot. He made good on the 15 yard shot he got that time.

The antlers on that 15-pointer are much darker than those of other bucks Mitch has bagged and had barbed wire tangled among the tines. Since this particular buck preferred rubbing his antlers on pine trees, the rack was probably stained by the sap. Mitch said he once saw the buck demolish a pine tree in 20 seconds.

Dark antlered 15-point with barbed wire wrapped in rack that Rompola collected the year before his booner. (Photo courtesy Mitch Rompola)

Once Rompola was done deer hunting during 1984, he did some post season scouting to "pin the other buck's movements down." The effort paid off because the buck was using the same bedding ground during 1985. On the two occasions Mitch saw the buck during 1984, he thought it had 10 points. It may have, but by 1985 he confirmed the impressive rack had 12 points.

He got a good look at the whitetail during the first week of September when its antlers were still in velvet. The bowhunter was sneaking through a bedding area at the time and a flicker of movement from the deer's tail attracted his attention. He didn't know it was a buck at the time, but he froze and when the whitetail moved toward him he was in for a surprise as the rack came into view. The deer was as close as 35 yards.

"I realized he was more impressive than I thought he was at that point," Mitch said. "Then I knew he would make Boone and Crockett. He had everything it takes to make it. The rack extended two or three inches beyond the tips of his ears."

Mitch saw the record buck on four occasions during late October and early November of 1985 before he got him and on at least one of those evenings he could have taken a 35 to 40 yard shot. It wasn't a high percentage shot, however, so he waited for a better chance.

That chance came just before 8:00 a.m. on November 8th as the buck returned to his bedding area. It was 7:50 when Mitch heard the buck coming and it took him almost 10 minutes to get into position for a shot. A blowdown consisting of a pair of cedar trees and a white birch that had fallen, was his blind that morning.

The whitetail was no more than 12 yards away at one point, but he wasn't in the right place for a shot then. Mitch wanted to wait for the deer to be angling away before shooting and he also wanted the buck to stop. However, when it became obvious the buck was going to keep walking, Rompola drew and held on an opening the animal was about to enter. The deer was 16 yards away when the arrow passed through the chest cavity.

Oddly enough, Mitch said the buck stopped in response to the sound the arrow made hitting brush after exiting the whitetail's body, as though unaware it was hurt. But that realization soon hit home and the buck took off running. It made it 80 yards before going down and Mitch saw the animal drop. He didn't waste much time getting to the fallen trophy.

The impressive 12-pointer was only 4 1/2 years old. It had a dressed weight of 186 pounds. Inside spread of the antlers ended up being 22 1/8 inches after drying for 60 days. The left beam was 27 2/8 inches long and the right one measured 28 3/8 inches. Truly impressive antler development for a buck of that age.

Rompola shot that buck with a 72 pound pull compound bow with Bear limbs and a homemade handle. He doesn't like the large handles that most compound bows come with from the factory because his grip frequently changes after a long shooting session, which can affect accuracy. The handles he makes have holes for fingers to insure the bow will always be gripped in the same fashion.

Mitch's bow was equipped with a sight using crosshairs and a bow quiver, although he always removes the quiver when he reaches his stand. He hunted with 2219 aluminum arrows. Blazer broadheads have accounted for a couple of his book bucks, but he also uses Bear and Wasp heads.

His outer clothing usually consists of a one-piece flight suit in green or brown. Rompola frequently uses a face mask while hunting and wears rubber boots both for walking through water and to reduce the amount of scent he leaves. Everything he does helps make Mitch Rompola one of the state's best bowhunters. And if his plans for the 1994 season come together, he may be adding another buck to his tally that will rival and perhaps beat, the record setting trophy he took in 1985.

Mitch Rompola with his Boone and Crockett bow kill taken on November 8, 1985. (Photo courtesy Mitch Rompola)

Louis Roy, Jr. with Baraga County's best typical and, until recently, the rack was the U.P.'s highest scoring typical.

Chapter 6

Baraga County Bragging Rights

In a number of ways the 1987 gun deer season was one of the best ever for Louis Roy, Jr. from L'anse. He shot a buck on the second day of the season that not only ranks as the best to his credit, the whitetail wore the highest-scoring typical rack known taken in the state that year and qualified as a new regional record for the Upper Peninsula (U.P.). The massive 12-point antlers scored 184 7/8 after the required 60-day drying period, easily qualifying for state and national records.

Another 12-pointer was the previous U.P. record typical, with a score of 179 5/8. The late John Schmidt from Crystal Falls shot the buck wearing those antlers in Iron County way back in 1927. Schmidt's monster buck had a dressed weight of 323 pounds while Roy's whitetail dressed out at 228 pounds, which is still a big deer.

A second highlight of Roy's 1987 hunt was it was the first year his 16-year-old daughter Jeannette was a member of the family hunting party. And she got her first deer, a spikehorn. There's no question Louis was just as proud of his daughter and her kill as he was of his success.

As if that wasn't enough, that season was the first every member of the hunting party bagged bucks, all seven of them. The other five members of the group were Louis' two brothers, Dennis and Tom; a cousin, Chuck Harris from Maryland; Louis Roy, Sr.; and Jeannette's boyfriend, Sean Wirtz. The big buck Louis shot was actually his second deer, having taken a smaller one opening day, so the party accounted for a total of eight bucks during gun season.

The Roys have always hunted as a family and they manage to have a good time regardless of how many deer they tag. The fact that they did so well that year made their hunt extra special, if not downright extraordinary, and certainly memorable. Their best season up until then was in 1985 when only four of them were hunting (Louis, Sr. and his three sons) and they took three bucks for a 75 percent success ratio. That season was the only one Chuck wasn't able to travel to the U.P. to hunt deer with them since 1978. Besides Chuck, all members of the 1987 hunting party live in or near L'anse.

They hunt on land open to the public in Baraga County. It was 1982 when they first hunted the property they did so well on during their most memorable fall and they learned a little more about the real estate every year since then. Many U.P. residents hunt deer in basically the same way the Roys do. They hunt from blinds, putting apples out nearby to feed deer that are in the area.

Louis, Jr. hunted a remote location four miles from a drivable road during 1987 for the first time. He originally found the spot during 1986 and planned to post there that season, but a hernia and surgery to correct it, changed his plans that year. His stand site overlooked a saddle in a hardwood ridge, with swamps on both sides of the ridge. The saddle was obviously a popular travel route for deer that crossed the ridge from one swamp to the other, evident by a well worn trail.

Louis saw something else during October of 1987 that renewed his interest in watching the saddle. There was a large circular patch of trampled ground where two bucks had fought. Sean helped Louis put a blind together on top of a 30-foot rock face on one side of the saddle. The other side of the saddle had a gradual uphill slope and the hardwood trees on that slope provided good visibility.

Jeannette and Sean hunted together from one blind. The pair originally picked a stand site within view of a logging road, but her father suggested they change spots to reduce the chances of being disturbed by other hunters. Louis led Sean 150 yards from the end of a logging road and asked, "How about here Sean?"

The words were barely out of his mouth when a deer jumped up and took off. Without hesitation, Sean gave his approval to the new site, and it proved to be a good one. Sean and Jeannette each shot a buck from the blind they built there and they saw three others that got away.

It hadn't been light long on opening day when they saw their first buck, but it left before they were able to get a shot. About 8:15 a.m. another buck, a forkhorn, appeared next to the blind. It was so close Sean could see it, but the blind blocked the deer from Jeannette's view. The antlered whitetail finally walked into the open and they both took shots at it, but missed.

They were baffled by how they both could have missed the forkhorn, but a thorough check of the area turned up no blood or hair and the animal simply didn't act like it had been hit either. They were back in the blind discussing what could have happened to their shots when still another buck appeared. This one had six points. Jeannette shot again with her 20 gauge shotgun, but that buck also got away. She shot slugs out of the gun before deer season opened and hit where she aimed, but was obviously having trouble placing her shots properly on deer.

They returned to their blind in the afternoon and an 8-point buck showed up then. Sean dropped it with one shot from his .30-30.

The following day, Jeannette exchanged the shotgun she had been using for one of her father's rifles, a .243. A spikehorn appeared in the distance at 7:35 a.m., but was edgy and hung back for at least 30 minutes before finally approaching the blind where Jeannette and Sean were anxiously waiting. When almost in position for a shot, the yearling buck stopped behind a tree where it rubbed its antlers.

Jeannette was ready when the buck stepped in the open broadside. There were no problems this time. The whitetail died instantly when she squeezed the rifle's trigger.

The young woman said she initially developed an interest in hunting to spend time with Sean, but now that she's tried deer hunting, she really likes it. She was already looking forward to the 1988 season by the time the '87 hunt ended.

Sean and Jeannette's blind wasn't the only hot spot. Three more bucks were bagged from another blind where Louis, Sr. usually hunts. The eldest member of the party saw five bucks from his blind on opening day, however, they were all button bucks and antlerless deer aren't legal in Baraga County during gun season.

It was raining on the second day of the season so the senior hunter decided not to go out, but he invited Chuck to use his blind, and he took him up on the offer. Chuck saw a spikehorn from his stand on opening day, but passed it up, both because he didn't want to end his hunt so quickly and he hoped to tag a bigger buck. He did see a better buck at 2:30 p.m. on day number two.

This whitetail had an obvious rack and was coming directly at Chuck, so he couldn't move. After the buck got by him, Chuck raised his .308 rifle, taking a shot. The 7-pointer ran when hit, but Chuck found the deer piled up at the base of a cliff it fell off when it died.

Rain turned to snow by day number three and Louis, Sr. relinquished his blind to Chuck again. An even bigger buck made an appearance that day. The big 8-pointer winded the waiting hunter though and whirled to leave. Chuck took a shot as the deer went through an opening, but just grazed the whitetail. He and Dennis spent that evening and much of the next day trailing the buck in the snow to confirm the hit was a nonfatal one. The buck never laid down, indicating he wasn't hurt.

Louis, Sr. reclaimed his blind on the fifth day of the season. A 6-point buck eventually showed up that day and he anchored it on the spot with a head shot from his .44 caliber Ruger rifle. That was the first buck he shot in 13 or 14 years, making it a notable kill for the Roy clan. Roy, Sr. hunted each of those years, but not as seriously as he had in his younger days. He had shots at bucks during that span of time, but failed to connect.

The senior member of the hunting party claimed some big bucks in Baraga County in his day, including a couple with large 10 and 14-point racks. However, he never had the antlers measured, so he isn't sure what they would score. But he knows they weren't as massive as the rack worn by the buck his oldest son shot in 1987.

Dennis shot the third buck from his father's blind. It was the second Sunday or the eighth day of the season and around 3:00 p.m. when the 3-pointer walked into view 15 to 20 minutes after a doe with two fawns appeared. Dennis saw a buck from the blind the evening before, too, but it disappeared before a shot was possible. He saw a second buck on that same day while in his vehicle, but wasn't able to get a shot at that one either.

The 3-pointer was angling toward Dennis on the top edge of a hill when he shot with his .308. When hit, the buck rolled downhill. To Dennis' surprise, the whitetail got up and ran when at the bottom of the hill. He scored another hit with a second shot, but that still didn't stop the deer.

Dennis followed after the buck immediately, the presence of snow making it easy to see its tracks. He got within 50 feet of the injured deer at one point, but it scooted out of sight, preventing a finishing shot. It wasn't long before Dennis caught up to the buck for the second time and finished it with a neck shot at point blank range.

Puzzled by the distance the deer covered, he examined the carcass to determine where he hit it and discovered his shots broke front and rear legs on opposite sides. He was sure his scope's crosshairs were on the buck's chest when he shot the first time and the rifle was sighted in before the season. A later check of the scope's accuracy showed it was hitting 15 inches low. He remembered that he tripped and fell backwards while walking to his father's blind the previous morning and figured the scope was jarred off during that fall.

Under the circumstances, it was amazing Dennis hit that buck at all! He was obviously meant to get that deer to complete the family's grand slam.

Tom filled his tag on opening morning of gun season with a

Three generations of Roys with the bucks they bagged during the 1987 gun season. Louis' father is on his right and daughter Jeannette on his left.

spikehorn. The buck he shot is the same one Chuck passed up. The two weren't hunting far apart. Tom only had one day to hunt due to work.

It was 9:45 a.m. when Tom saw the whitetail and he thought it was a doe at first. Then he looked at the deer with the 3X-9X power scope mounted on his .30-06 and immediately saw spikes. When no more than 35 yards away and broadside, Tom aimed for a spot behind the buck's shoulder and fired.

The buck bounded twice and stopped. Concerned that he might have missed, Tom shot again, and the deer collapsed. There was no need to worry though. Both shots connected and, in fact, the holes from them were next to each other. Sometimes bucks just don't drop immediately, even when well hit with a powerful bullet.

Tom's spike was the second buck bagged by the party opening morning. It was 8:05 a.m. when Louis, Jr. saw a small 6-pointer. Rather than cross the saddle in the ridge, the buck came downhill into the saddle along the ridge. When the buck turned broadside, Louis fired a round from his bolt action .270. Although well hit, the whitetail covered 40 yards before going down.

If it weren't for the two deer bag limit in effect then during gun season, Louis' hunt would have been over as soon as he dropped the 6-point. He's glad he was able to continue hunting, however, he almost didn't hunt the second morning due to the rain. It was raining hard when he fixed breakfast at 5:00 a.m. and he considered not going afield because he was bound to get soaked during the four mile trip to his blind.

Then Louis found an old rain suit that would help keep him dry and he got to thinking he should be out there in case Jeannette and Sean needed help. They called upon him to field dress Sean's buck the evening before. His decision to hunt in the rain proved to be a wise one.

He arrived at his blind well before daylight (about 6:30 a.m.) and by 8:00 he started to feel a little disgusted by the lack of deer sightings. The buck he shot the day before was the only whitetail he saw. No does had been by. But he wasn't disgusted for long because that's when the book buck made his appearance.

"Oh my God," Louis remembers thinking when the buck walked into view. "I knew he was huge as soon as I saw him. He walked like he owned the woods.

"I didn't have time to think, just react. I saw him, grabbed the gun and shot him. The buck dropped right there and then I started shaking all over."

Louis couldn't move the buck until after it was gutted. A four wheeler was necessary to get the carcass out of the woods. Jeannette also bagged her buck that morning and when she saw her father she called out excitedly, "I got one! I got one!"

Then Louis asked his daughter what she thought of the buck he got. Her answer was, "Holy Wha, is he big!" All some of the other family members could say when first seeing the buck is "Wha!"

There were actually a total of three bucks taken by the group that rainy day. Chuck also scored. And that's not the only buck Louis shot in the rain. In 1985 he collected a nice 10-pointer that was his best buck until the booner, and it was raining hard when he shot it.

It was the evening of the third day of the season that year and he was using a .243 mounted with a scope. He had see-through mounts. When the buck appeared, Louis tried to aim with the scope, but the view was blurred by water droplets. He was able to align the rifle's iron sights by looking through the mounts and made a killing shot. Anyone who considers not going deer hunting on a rainy day should remember this group's results before deciding.

Interestingly, the rifle Louis shot his two bucks with during November of 1987 was an early Christmas present from his wife. She allowed him to pick out his present from a local gun shop during the second week of October. He entered the shop with the intention of selecting a rifle in 7 mm magnum, but the model in that caliber that he shouldered didn't fit. When he tried the .270, it "fit like a glove."

He shot the new rifle a lot before deer season opened in an

effort to familiarize himself with it. The practice obviously paid off. And he couldn't think of a better way to break the rifle in than taking the two bucks during its first season of use.

Why did this party do so well during the fall of 1987?

They felt the major factor responsible for their exceptional success was an increase in the local deer herd. The winter of 1986-87 was a record mild one in the U.P. Whitetail survival in the region during the previous winter was also good. DNR surveys showed the herd was up as much as 23 percent in the western U.P. during 1987.

Ages of the bucks bagged by the party reflects an increasing population with lots of yearlings. Five of the seven whitetails were yearlings (1 1/2 years old). The fact that three of those five had racks rather than spikes is probably a result of the previous mild winter.

Sean's buck was 2 1/2 years old and Louis' booner was 5 1/2.

Chuck added extra incentive for every one in the group to be successful during that most memorable fall. He brought hats with him designed for deer hunters inscribed with, "Go Ahead Buck, Make My Day." He told them they couldn't have their hats, however, until they got their deer. Every one got their hat and you will notice most of them are wearing their hats in photos accompanying this chapter.

A very successful deer hunting family. From left to right are Dennis, Chuck, Louis Sr., Louis Jr., Jeannette, Sean and Tom.

Doug Palomaki of Negaunee with 22-point nontypical be bagged with a muzzleloader in Marquette County during December of 1987.

Chapter 7

Black Powder Buck To Remember

Doug Palomaki from Negaunee has some specific goals as a deer hunter. He wants to shoot "scorable bucks" (those measuring at least 140 inches) with his bow, centerfire rifle and muzzleloading rifle. He also plans on tagging a Boone and Crockett (B&C) buck, hopefully with bow and arrow, as well as a whitetail with a state record rack.

Read on before judging how realistic those goals might be.

Palomaki came closer to one of his goals during 1987 by bagging a scorable buck with his muzzleloader, which was his third whitetail with the front loading rifle. He already had a scorable buck to his credit with bow and arrow that he took during 1980. The 11-point bow kill scored 141 7/8. The black powder buck he got on December 5, 1987 actually came close to achieving two of his goals at the same time. It was almost a state record.

The nontypical 22-point rack scored 180 7/8, according to Commemorative Bucks of Michigan (CBM), the state's big game record keeper. The current state record nontypical rack taken with a muzzleloader has 23 points and a score of 185 5/8. Robert Gendron bagged the buck that grew those antlers in Hillsdale County during 1977. Another nontypical with 17 points and scoring 185, was shot with a muzzleloader by Warren Vogler in Washtenaw County during 1983, putting Palomaki's buck in the number three position in that category at the time he got it. The head now ranks fifth due to a couple of larger bucks taken since then.

Although Doug is pleased with the buck he got with his musket, he saw another one that would have met one or two of his toughest goals, if he could have gotten it.

"I feel we've got the state record where we hunt," he said when I interviewed him. "In fact, I think I saw him this year (1987), believe it or not."

Doug was bowhunting during early November at the time he saw the buck. He said the whitetail's typical antlers had 12 points with 15-inch tines and a 26 to 28-inch spread. He estimated its weight at 280 pounds.

"I thought it was a cow coming through," Doug said. "This was a tremendous deer!"

The buck came no closer than 40 yards, so Doug didn't get a shot at it. He refuses to take a bad shot. In fact, he only releases an arrow when he knows he can make a clean kill, and he's never lost a deer he's hit for that reason.

By the way, Doug has somewhat of an idea what a 280 pound whitetail should look like because he shot one that had a live weight of 260 pounds with a centerfire rifle in 1983. His 11-point bow kill had antlers that were 23 inches wide and he knows they would easily fit inside the rack of the record book buck he didn't shoot at.

Antlers from that big buck would have met B&C minimums (170) with no problem and, as Doug said, the rack might have scored high enough to set a new state record. The current state record typical score, according to CBM, is 186 1/8. The buck that grew that rack was bagged by Mark Ritchie in 1984 and is covered in another chapter in this book.

That booner Doug didn't get and the 22-pointer he shot, were two of 22 different bucks he saw during 1987 hunting seasons. He tagged one other buck with his bow, an 8-pointer with an 18 1/2-inch spread. He passed that buck up on five different occasions before finally taking it on November 8th.

Although 1987 was a good year, he didn't see as many bucks as the year before. Doug counted 28 different bucks during the fall of 1986.

A number of factors are responsible for this deer hunter's phenomenal success. Of prime importance is his unique character, philosophy and dedication that have evolved over the years he has hunted deer, making him a true trophy buck hunter. He's primarily a bow hunter and hunts every day of the season.

He teaches Industrial Arts at a local high school and is done work by 2:30 p.m. every day during the week, which enables him to hunt every evening. The area he hunts is a 40 minute drive from his home in Marquette County, another plus in enabling him to hunt day in and day out. More on the area Doug hunts later.

As a big buck hunter, Palomaki hunts day-after-day with no intention of shooting a deer, although he has opportunities to kill bucks many of the days he hunts. On most occasions he's content to "monitor" bucks to learn more about their behavior and size them up. He also spends a lot of time scouting, examining buck sign and preparing new stands for later hunting.

Doug doesn't actually like to consider killing a buck until November 1, a month after bow season opens. By then, he has a good idea how big many of the bucks are and where his chances are best of getting a look at, and maybe a shot, at a dominant buck. Dominant bucks are the only ones he's interested in shooting, and he said there's only about 10 days during the fall that he has a chance of getting one of those bucks.

The days on which Doug consistently sees dominant bucks are October 24-26, November 3-6, November 15-18, around Thanksgiving and the first couple of days of muzzleloader season in December. If he had to pick one day out of the year he could hunt deer, it would be November 6th. On that day during the four-year period from 1984 through 1987 he had seen an 11-point, 10-point, two 12s and 14-point bucks.

It was November 6, 1987 when he saw that impressive B&C buck. It was also on that day during 1980 that he bow-bagged that 11-pointer scoring 141 7/8. That buck weighed 220 pounds and was aged at 7 1/2 years old. Doug knew the buck was around, but the day he shot him was the only time he saw him.

"I don't have to see a buck to hunt him," he said. "The dominant bucks you seldom see. I feel if I see a scoring buck once a year, I'm doing well. And if I can get a shot at him, that's the second plus."

Doug keeps tabs on dominant bucks through the sign they leave, scrapes, rubs and tracks. He's found that most of the large primary scrapes made by dominant bucks are rectangular in shape rather than circular, and these scrapes are often near large rubs. Big-racked bucks frequently rub their antlers on large diameter trees. One of the largest trees Palomaki has seen rubbed by a buck was a cedar tree 20 inches in diameter.

Big bucks leave big tracks, too. Doug has seen prints more than six inches in length. He looks at how bucks place their feet to distinguish the prints of an old buck from those of a young one. Big tracks on which prints from front and rear feet are exactly on top of one another were made by a young buck. Imprints from rear hooves will appear 1/4 to 1/2-inch behind those made by front feet, in tracks made by mature bucks. Older bucks also tend to be bow-legged, according to Palomaki, with their toes pointed slightly inward.

Doug does a lot of serious scouting during March and April, little or none during the summer and continues scouting during the fall. Due to his familiarity with the location of primary scrapes made by dominant bucks, he often opens them before the deer do, simply clearing the ground on the first couple of visits and adding a few drops of doe-in-heat scent the next couple of times. Bucks usually take the scrapes over within a week.

Palomaki frequently positions stands near primary scrapes, but also puts apples out to add to the attractiveness of the site during early fall. By late November, he switches to cedar as bait. When bowhunting from tree stands, Doug likes to be over 20 feet high and uses fox urine as a cover scent, ordering a gallon every year.

As a general rule, Doug alternates stands on a daily basis to reduce disturbance at any one spot, but there are exceptions to this, based on current conditions and deer activity. He said he has about a dozen portable tree stands that he uses for bowhunting throughout the fall. Palomaki only hunts one of his more remote locations four times a year, always with bow and arrow. He has to walk 3/4-of-a-mile through water to reach this stand, wearing hip boots.

Doug had logged a total of 280 hours on that stand through 1987 without releasing an arrow, but he had passed up a lot of bucks there.

"That's where I'm planning on getting a nice buck," he said. "Out of those four days each year, I've seen an 8-pointer and 10-pointer fight within two days of one another each year. They will fight within a one or two-day period every year."

Doug described the fight between those two bucks that he witnessed on October 25, 1985. The 8-pointer was already nearby when the 10-point appeared and spotted his rival. He said the newcomer moved toward his adversary in a half circle, hitting about 20 trees with his antlers enroute.

"I was scared and I was up about 25 feet," Doug confessed. "He was really hammering on those trees. When the 10 reached the 8, they just connect racks and push and shove a little bit. Then the 8-pointer breaks off and he comes over and starts rubbing trees, while the 10-pointer goes back to where he was.

"After rubbing a tree, the 8-pointer starts toward the apples. The 10-pointer turns with the hair standing up on his back and walks over to the 8, who really has his hair up! They glared at each other then connect racks. The 10 grabs the 8 and pushes him backwards about three times. Then they disconnect and pause for a second.

"When they reconnect, the 10 lifts the 8 right off of his feet and twists his head, flipping the 8 over sideways. They were on a little knoll and the 8 skidded downhill. When he stood up he went baaaa, baaaa as if to say, 'Uncle, Uncle,' and then walked off."

Doug could have shot either of those bucks for three years in a row - 1984, 1985 and 1986 - but decided to pass them up. He saw them again during 1987 and felt the 10-pointer had a good enough rack, he would take him. However, the buck didn't give him an opportunity for a good bow shot that time.

Palomaki does some rattling and also uses grunt calls. He uses three different grunt calls to vary the tone. The ones he owns are made by Knight and Hale, Lohman and Noel Feather. Young bucks have responded best to Palomaki's grunting. In terms of rattling, he does it sparingly, about 10 times a year when conditions are right. Doug has rattled in four or five bucks he could have shot, but didn't.

One quiet evening during early November, for example, Doug rattled once when there was 12 minutes of shooting light left.

"I just put the antlers down and a nice 10-pointer came in like he wanted to get shot, and stood around for the longest time wondering what was going on. He was probably shootable, but if he came in that easy, I figured next year he'll come again. What happens is if I rattle in a buck, I'll be so satisfied I won't go back to that stand."

Where Doug hunts has a lot to do with the type of deer hunter he is. He hunts on 37 forties (about three square miles) of private property. He is one of seven or eight guys who own the large chunk of land, but most of them aren't serious deer hunters. Palomaki had been hunting the property seriously for 15 years by 1987, but had been going there since 1960.

The bulk of the land is composed of cedar swamps with islands of hardwood trees. Doug does most of his hunting along the edges of hardwood islands. Due to limited hunting pressure, deer aren't as spooky there as they would be on public land visited by lots of hunters. Even more important though, is the fact that the hunters who own the land such as Doug, can and do control the buck harvest for the production of trophy animals.

"Basically, we take spikes and mature bucks," Doug said. "We let the forks, sixes and small eights go. We shoot a lot of spikehorns, but will not shoot a forkhorn.

"Two years ago rifle season (1986), I saw a buck every day of rifle season. The first day, I saw three bucks and didn't shoot any of them. The last day of rifle season I finally shot a buck. I had a spike, fork and a six come in. The six had a broken beam. I shot the spikehorn."

Doug ended up shooting the 6-point that had the broken beam with his bow a year later - November of 1987. By then the buck had an 8-point rack with an 18 1/2-inch spread.

Palomaki's hunting party has a rule against shooting does, and the reason for that is he feels there is an even sex ratio on the property. He said if you see four deer, two of them will be bucks. Doug understands the importance of harvesting does from herds where there are more of them than bucks.

The harvest strategy Doug and his friends use on their land insures bucks will live long enough to grow large racks. Adequate nutrition and the proper genetics for antler growth are also present, based on bucks the property has produced. It's an ideal situation for big buck hunting.

The 22-pointer Doug ended up shooting during December of 1987 was seen on three different occasions before then, each time during early November of 1987. Doug saw the buck twice himself and his son Jim saw it once. Jim and Doug were bowhunting one morning around November 6th and Jim was supposed to pick Doug up from his stand around noon.

Jim was on the way to meet his father and was only about 50 yards from their pickup truck when he saw a movement that proved to be the buck. He put some fox urine on as cover scent and tried to stalk the whitetail. Jim managed to keep the buck in sight for 1 1/2 hours, but never got in position for a good bow shot.

Three days earlier, Doug saw the same buck and he sighted it one more time after dark as he was driving back to camp and the animal stood along the road. The buck was with three does that night and one of them was odd looking, built low to the ground. Each of the three times the buck was seen though, he was judged to be a 10-pointer. The numerous nontypical points were not identified.

Efforts to get a shot at that buck during bow season failed, and he wasn't seen at all during rifle season. It was the second day of Muzzleloader season before Doug saw the deer again, but he was actually trying for a different buck at the time that he had never seen, but he felt it had a better rack, based on its tracks and rubs. He saw 15 or 20 deer that evening, including three bucks he passed up before the 22-pointer arrived - a spike, fork and an eight.

Then Doug saw the same three does that were with the big buck when he got a glimpse of it after dark. He recognized the odd-looking doe right away.

"When I saw those three does come in I said, 'That big buck has got to be with them. I just know he is.'

"It wasn't, but three to five minutes later when I looked, here he comes up the deer run. He was off on the edge of a field about 150 yards away. It looked like a shootable buck. 'Geez that's a dandy,' I thought to myself. I put up my binoculars for a closer look and said, 'Oh boy, that sure is!'"

At that point, Doug grabbed his .50 caliber muzzleloader loaded with 105 grains of black powder and a round ball, and cocked the hammer.

"He was coming through a small field with some bushes and trees. He would stop behind every bush, every rock and every tree. He was smart. This was taking five to 10 minutes, but there was plenty of shooting light left.

"He was coming to a point where the run split in three directions and I decided I would have to take him before he got to that intersection, for the best shot. There was a bush just before the trail branched and he stopped behind it, looking at those does feeding for three or four minutes."

The pressure was beginning to build. There have been other times when Doug saw dominant bucks come in so far then suddenly turn and leave with no apparent reason. He had the crosshairs of the four power scope mounted on his musket covering the buck and decided to shoot when it took a step ahead or if it turned to look back, a sign a buck is about to vacate the premises. Then Palomaki started worrying about the rifle firing.

"I hope that cap goes off after all this," he was thinking. "You know how muzzleloaders are? They're kinda moody at times. It was loaded on Friday and this was Saturday.

"He takes the one step and I said, 'This is it. Oh, I hope this cap goes off. This is a dandy buck.' Even then, I thought he was a 10, 11 or 12."

The buck was 40 to 45 yards away and broadside when Doug squeezed the trigger and the rifle went off, with the resulting smoke screen temporarily blocking his view of the deer. The whitetail ran off after being hit and Palomaki was sure he heard him crash to the ground. But he got concerned when he could not find any blood. There was snow though and Doug was able to follow the buck's running tracks to where it piled up. There proved to be no blood at all on the snow any where.

As soon as Doug reached the fallen buck he was sure the antlers were scorable, but was surprised to see it was a nontypical.

"I kinda smiled when I saw it was a nontypical," he said, "because I figure in the next couple of years we're going to have some more nontypicals. That buck had time to spread his genes around."

The buck had a dressed weight of 170 pounds and is thought to have been 3 1/2 or 4 1/2 years old.

"I wish I could have waited another year or two to get him," Doug commented. "On a buck like that though, you just can't wait. You can't let 'em all go!"

If you ask me, I think Doug Palomaki has an excellent chance of reaching most of his goals as a deer hunter, and I wouldn't be surprised to hear more big buck tales from him in the future. But even if he doesn't accomplish all of his goals, I bet he has a lot of fun trying, and that's what deer hunting is all about!

Patrick Flanagan with 24-point nontypical he got during 1990 after missing it the year before.

Chapter 8

Huron County Giant

Soon after legal shooting time on opening morning of Michigan's 1989 gun season, Patrick Flanagan from Livonia got a shot at a whitetail buck in Huron County that was wearing a huge nontypical rack.

"I knew it was a big nontypical," Flanagan said. "his rack looked like hay forks coming through the woods, but nobody would believe me."

Unfortunately, the buck got away and no one else saw the deer, so there was no way for him to verify his story. Not then anyway. He got another chance to prove he knew what he was talking about on opening day of the 1990 season and he made good on that opportunity. Now he can show anyone who doubted his word that he knows what he saw that morning.

Flanagan bagged a buck with the largest rack known taken in the state during 1990 seasons and it was indeed a nontypical. The antlers have a total of 24 points and a final official score of 215 5/8, according to Commemorative Bucks of Michigan (CBM). The rack ranks 7th among nontypicals on CBM's alltime records list.

Paul Mickey from Kawkawlin bagged a buck with the largest nontypical rack on record for the state in Bay County during 1976. The massive antlers have a total of 29 points and an amazing final score of 238 2/8. Mickey saw the enormous nontypical buck twice while bowhunting during the fall of 1976 before finally killing it with a rifle in late November. He made the shot from 200 yards after spotting the whitetail feeding in a winter wheat field at a distance of 700 yards and stalking closer.

Paul Mickey with Michigan's highest scoring nontypical, a 29-pointer measuring 238 2/8 that he shot in Bay County during 1976.

That's not the only entry Paul has in state records. He has seven other listings for Bay County, all of which were taken with bow and arrow, including another nontypical with 17 points that scores 184 3/8. He also has taken five record book bucks from Schoolcraft County, including a 10-point typical scoring 169 4/8 he got with a rifle in 1988, but that's another story.

Flanagan's buck is only the third nontypical recorded for Huron County, according to the 3rd edition of <u>Michigan Big Game Records</u>, CBM's third state record book. The book contains a county-by-county listing for deer records. All of the bucks that qualify for state records are listed under the county they were taken in regardless of whether they were bagged with centerfire gun, muzzleloader or bow and arrow. Separate record lists that are also printed in the book are maintained for rifle/shotgun, handgun, muzzleloader and bow kills.

Huron County, by the way, is at the top of the state's "thumb" northeast of Bay City. There's a lot of farming in the county with corn and sugar beets being two of the main crops.

A 25-point nontypical scoring more than Flanagan's was shot in Huron County during 1876 by an unknown hunter. Those antlers measured 222 4/8. An 18-point nontypical scoring 165 1/8 was taken in the county during 1982 by Jane Western. So it had been 115 years since a buck of exceptional proportions had been taken from Huron County, according to state records.

Flanagan wishes it would have only been 114 years. He's disappointed about not getting the big nontypical during 1989. He realizes he made a mistake on November 15, 1989 that cost him that buck and he doesn't plan on making that mistake again.

Centerfire rifles aren't permitted for deer hunting in Huron County, just shotguns, muzzleloaders and handguns. Flanagan uses a Remington Model 1100 shotgun in 12 gauge that has a 3-inch chamber. The barrel has an improved cylinder choke, which is best suited for shooting slugs. However, Patrick said he carries both slugs and buckshot. The buckshot loads are used when walking ditches for shots at bucks that are jumped.

When Flanagan loaded his gun on opening day of the 1989 season, he put 00 buckshot in the chamber, even though he knew he was planning on posting for a while first thing in the morning. He took up a position behind some trees where he could watch a small woods on property owned by a relative. He didn't have to wait long for the big buck to appear. It came walking by at a brisk pace.

When the whitetail was less than 20 yards away, Flanagan fired. The buck went down, but quickly got back up and took off running. Patrick tried to connect with slugs that were behind the buckshot as the deer vacated the premises, but saw no signs of a hit.

"I followed after that buck for a long ways," Flanagan said, "and I couldn't find any blood. In the excitement of the moment, I think I shot high. One of the pellets must have grazed him. I would have had a better chance of getting that buck then if my first shot would have been with a slug rather than buckshot."

Patrick had been hunting that piece of property for about five years and the buck he missed during 1989 was the biggest, by far, he had seen there. In fact, before then he was convinced there weren't any big bucks in the area. He always saw a lot of deer, but they were mostly does. The bucks he saw were small.

Flanagan had shot two deer on the property previously. One was a doe and the other was a 7-point buck. He admits that he's not one of the state's most serious deer hunters, but he did have a hand in the shooting of another trophy buck.

That was during 1950. He was 14 years old then and it was his first year of deer hunting. He was hunting in Ogemaw County with Charles Wilson, his father's friend. They were both in the same blind early in the morning on opening day when a big buck appeared in front of the blind.

"We both shot at the same time," Patrick remembered. "I thought I hit the deer and so did he, but when you're a boy, you don't argue with your elders."

They were both shooting .32 special Winchester rifles, so it probably would have been tough to accurately determine who actually got the deer anyway. Wilson tagged the deer, which had antlers carrying 22 points. Those antlers were never measured, but Flanagan said a CBM measurer was in the process of trying to locate the rack so it can be scored and entered in state records.

Flanagan continued hunting deer until he was 19 or 20 without tagging a buck of his own. By then he got interested in duck hunting. All of his hunting time was devoted to the pursuit of waterfowl over the next 23 years. It wasn't until 1980 that Patrick got back into deer hunting.

For about five years he hunted out of the Birch Lodge at Trout Lake in the U.P. The death of the lodge's owner forced Flanagan to hunt deer elsewhere and that's when he started opening the season on private property in Huron County. He didn't shoot any whitetails in the U.P., so all of his kills had been in Huron County. The monster he claimed in 1990 was his third deer from the county.

Patrick said there were a number of reasons that prompted him to hunt the same spot during 1990 that he had hunted during 1989. At the top of the list, of course, was the chance that he would see the big nontypical again. If the animal was still alive, and Flanagan felt it was, the whitetail might follow the same route it had the year before.

He may have seen the big buck before gun season opened, but he'll never know for sure. A river flows through the property where Flanagan shot his record book buck and he regularly float hunts for ducks on the river from a canoe. He said it's not unusual to see deer along the river.

"One day I saw a big deer from the canoe. It was a big, big deer, but all I saw was the back and tail. I never got a look at the head."

During the summer, Patrick saw some deer using the woods where he missed the giant buck.

"I knew there were three deer back there," he said. "I saw them from a distance, so I couldn't tell what they were. I didn't want to disturb them, so I didn't try to get closer for a better look."

Flanagan knew one of the whitetails in the area might be the one he missed during 1989 and that was good enough for him. At daybreak on November 15, 1990 he was positioned behind the same trees that screened him the year before. This time a slug was in the chamber of his shotgun.

It gets light about 7:00 a.m. at that time of year. At 7:10 Patrick saw a doe approaching and a buck was right behind her. It wasn't the nontypical though. A respectable 8 or 10-point typical rack adorned the trailing whitetail's head.

Before the buck was in position for a shot, a third whitetail appeared off to the side of the other two. This one was also a buck and it was the one Flanagan was hoping to see. He held his fire until the trophy animal was within 30 yards. Three slugs were required to put the buck down.

"I was glad I saw the big one before the first buck was close enough for a shot," Patrick said. "I would have shot the 8 or 10-pointer if the other buck hadn't shown up."

The buck's antlers weren't all that was big. Minus the head and hide, the carcass weighed 190 pounds. The dressed weight would have been well in excess of 200 pounds if the hide and head had been attached when it was weighed.

The rack's gross score was 227 1/8. Deductions amounted to 11 4/8, putting the official final tally at 215 5/8. The antlers had a total of 56 3/8 inches of nontypical points, including a couple of drop tines on each beam. Long typical tines helped boost the score, too. The brow tine on the left beam was especially long.

Beam lengths were 24 4/8 inches on the right and 21 3/8 inches on the left. Inside spread between the beams was 17 6/8 inches.

Interestingly, the county's highest scoring typical is a 13-pointer measuring 152 1/8 that was also bagged during 1990. Harley Marseilles from Frankenmuth was the lucky hunter. He connected on that whitetail at 8:30 a.m. on November 15th, not long after Flanagan got his nontypical. Marseilles' buck had a dressed weight of 225 pounds.

Those who questioned Patrick Flanagan's credibility and/or his eyesight after opening day of 1989 have long since realized he really did know what he was talking about when he mentioned missing a huge nontypical. He's got the proof hanging on his wall. However, he's also very fortunate the whitetail gave him the opportunity for a replay so he could disprove his critics. It doesn't always happen that way in deer hunting.

Mike Fitzgerald with his Boone and Crockett bow kill from Jackson County that he took while scrape hunting. (Photo courtesy Mike Fitzgerald)

Chapter 9

Scrape Hunting Know How

Mike Fitzgerald from Jackson put himself in a unique group during the fall of 1990 when he bagged a buck with the highest scoring antlers taken by a bowhunter for the year. He was only the fifth archer in the state's history to collect a buck with a rack large enough to qualify for listing in Boone and Crockett (B&C) Records, according to CBM. The 11-pointer he arrowed on November 11, 1990 in Jackson County scored an even 170, equaling the minimum necessary for B&C entry of typical whitetails.

Over the years, Michigan has produced plenty of B&C bucks, but the vast majority have been claimed by gun hunters. The fact that bowhunters had only accounted for five booners compared to roughly 65 tagged by hunters using firearms, indicates how tough an accomplishment it is. In fact, just about as many B&C qualifiers had been killed by vehicles on the state's roads as by archers.

Although the odds of getting such a unique buck with bow and arrow are not high, they favor serious bowhunters like Fitzgerald. He hunts whitetails with archery equipment exclusively and he hunts hard during bow season, usually managing to get out five or six days a week. Mike said he had been bowhunting for deer 13 years by 1990 and had 16 of them to his credit besides the book buck he got that fall. Ten or 12 of the whitetails among that total number were bucks, including three 8-pointers.

The minimum score for entry of typical bow kills in state records is 100. Typical antlered bucks bagged with a bow that measure a minimum of 125 qualify for national records maintained by the Pope and Young Club. Pope and Young only records big game bagged with bow and arrow. Most of B&C's entries are bagged with firearms, but bucks taken with archery equipment that meet their higher minimums are also eligible.

The other archers besides Fitzgerald who bagged B&C bucks in Michigan through 1990 are Mitch Rompola, Craig Calderone, Nick Converse and Robert Savola. Previous chapters were devoted to Rompola and Calderone. Converse, who lives in Livingston County, got a 10-pointer scoring 178 1/8 on November 9, 1987. The buck was practically in his back yard when he got it.

Nick said his wife saw the buck bed down in a swale behind the house and it was still there when he got home from work. Converse called his brother and they both circled around to a fenceline in an effort to get a shot at the buck. His brother stayed near the end of the fenceline with a set of rattling antlers as Nick moved closer.

There was a smaller buck and a doe in the area, too, and when Nick's brother rattled, the big boy got up and started fighting with the second buck, chasing it off. The booner then laid down again. Nick kept a pine tree between himself and the buck, stalking to within 35 yards, making a killing shot with his 68 pound pull Bear Kodiak Magnum bow.

Savola is the first person in the state known to have taken a B&C buck with bow and arrow and he was only 14 years old at the time. He was living with his parents in their rural Alger County home and the story about how he got the 10-pointer is similar to Converse's. It was the evening of December 8, 1981 when Savola got the book buck.

The whitetail simply showed up to feed on apples that fell from trees in the Savola's yard. The previous evening, Robert's father missed the same buck with three arrows. Measurements of the antlers totaled 170 7/8.

Fitzgerald's favorite tactic for scoring on bucks with a bow is scrape hunting and that's what he was doing when he got his B&C buck. He said he looks for fresh scrapes, especially large ones that measure four or five feet across, and sets up in a tree within bow range. The booner was approaching one of those five-footers when Mike's arrow ended his interest in does.

The big one was the second buck Mike got while scrape hunting during 1990. He shot a 4-point on the first or second day of November while employing the technique in a different area.

"I found a scrape that had been hit two days in a row and I figured the buck would be back," Mike said. "I set up 15 yards from the scrape on the edge of a cornfield and woods. The tracks by the scrape weren't real big, so when the 4-point showed up I figured he had to be the one doing the scraping. I shot when he was 10 yards away and the broadhead went through his backbone. He dropped right there."

Mike said he was hunting from a homemade portable, strap-on tree stand when he got the forkhorn. The stand was 10 feet off the ground and the wind was in his favor. He said he pays a lot of attention to wind direction when deciding where to ambush a buck. He won't hunt a spot if the wind isn't right.

He feels paying attention to the wind is more important then using scents, either attractants or types designed to cover human odor. In fact, he's never used any kind of scent. The scrapes he hunts are effective enough at attracting bucks.

The second thing Fitzgerald is careful about besides wind direction is trying not to over hunt a spot.

" I try not to hunt the same spot two days in a row," he said. "It doesn't take deer long to catch onto you if you keep going to the same place. If I want to hunt a spot again, I try to wait four days or so before going back."

Mike had been hunting with a PSE Jet Flight Express bow set at 60 pounds for three or four years and that's what he shot both of his bucks with in 1990. He uses Easton XX75 arrows tipped with two-blade Zwickey broadheads. Mike said he's used the same type of broadhead since he started bowhunting.

He doesn't use sights, shooting instinctively with fingers. He uses the Apache draw with three fingers on the string under his arrow, which allows him to look down the shaft. Uncle Ben Stachowicz from Jackson got Mike started bowhunting, who in turn, was introduced to the sport by veteran archer Jack Hunter. Jack started bowhunting for deer in the 1930s. All three of them used to hunt together, but Hunter passed away a number of years ago.

To maintain accuracy and proficiency with his instinctive shooting style, Fitzgerald tries to shoot year-round. He goes through practice sessions a few times a week.

Like most deer hunters, Mike got his introduction to deer hunting during gun season and started bowhunting soon afterward. He hunted with both gun and bow for a couple of years, then quit hunting with firearms. The number of hunters in the field during the gun hunt and a bad experience with an individual interfering with a deer he shot, turned him off on firearms season.

The first whitetail Mike got with a bow was a "little spikehorn." He shot it on opening day of the 1978 season during the evening.

"That deer kinda surprised me," Fitzgerald said. "I shot him through the lungs like you're supposed to and I expected him to run out of sight. He only went 10 feet and fell over dead."

Mike was impressed with the effectiveness of a sharp broadhead. He was also hooked for life on bowhunting for deer. The challenge of successfully collecting a deer with bow and arrow, companionship with his uncle and limited vacation time contributed to his dedication to bowhunting.

He and his uncle usually spend two weeks during October bowhunting in the U.P. and most of the rest of his time is spent hunting near home. Mike said he's seen a couple of dandy bucks in the U.P. that would probably score in the 150s, but he hadn't been fortunate enough to connect on one of the Upper's big bucks yet. By November, when scrapes start appearing with regularity, Fitzgerald gets serious about buck hunting.

A grunt call helped him connect on one of the three 8-pointers to his credit on the evening of November 14, 1989. Mike was positioned 18 yards from a five-foot wide scrape when he blew the call.

"He heard it and came stormin' in," Fitzgerald remembered. "He came right under my tree and I couldn't shoot. Then he went to the scrape and I got him."

Mike said the buck had just made the scrape that morning and he felt it would be back to check it later in the day. He was right. Even without the call, he probably would have seen that buck.

Fitzgerald was following the blood trail of a forkhorn he shot one morning during the first week of November in 1987 when he got another 8-point. He and his uncle were hunting along the Grand River at the time and Mike had both of his bow tags with him. Mike was trailing the forkhorn while his uncle made a loop toward the river and Stachowicz apparently jumped the bigger buck. Fitzgerald was motionless as the buck approached.

"I dropped to my knees when I saw the buck coming," Mike related. "We were eye-to-eye for a while, but he couldn't tell what I was. I drew my bow as soon as he turned his head. I didn't have much time."

The archer put an arrow through the buck's lungs as it angled away at a distance of 22 yards. It didn't take him long to find that deer. By the time he and his uncle resumed tracking the forkhorn, however, two other bowhunters had recovered the buck. Mike saw them loading the carcass in a boat and they soon took off with the whitetail.

In terms of camouflage clothing, Mike said he either wears garments featuring a standard green/brown pattern or green coveralls. He prefers camo clothes made of material that is soft and quiet such as chamois. His foot wear varies, depending on the circumstances. Mike said he frequently wears rubber-bottomed boots to minimize his scent and he occasionally wears hip boots when hunting wet, swampy terrain. He sometimes wears leather boots if going to an area where he's not concerned about leaving his scent where he walks.

Large deer tracks are what led Mike to his B&C buck. At least that sign is what initially got him interested in the location where he got the book buck. The tracks were the biggest he had ever seen in the area. He saw fresh prints from the buck every three or four days.

Trees torn up by the buck's antlers appeared later, followed by big scrapes. The scrapes were close to the junction of a weed field and a small patch of corn near the edge of a wet swamp. Soon after Mike got the 4-pointer, he spent an evening in his tree stand watching one of those big scrapes.

Late in the day, two bucks emerged from the swamp together. Mike said one of the bucks only had a single antler carrying three big points. The second buck had both antlers, complete with long tines.

He said he thought it was strange to see the bucks together since the rut was getting underway. At any rate, the whitetails did some sparring then separated. The half-racked buck came to within 20 yards and Mike could have taken him, but he waited, hoping for a shot at the bigger animal.

The trophy whitetail stayed out of range though, milling around in the corn patch. It never got any closer than 40 yards and Mike doesn't like to shoot that far. A week and a half later, Fitzgerald was in the same stand and the buck he wanted reappeared a half hour before dark. The whitetail was by himself this time and he gave Mike a 25 yard, quartering away shot as he walked toward the scrape.

"I figured he would score high," the bowhunter said, referring to the buck's antlers, "but I didn't really think about the size of his rack then. I just tried to get a shot."

His arrow nicked one lung and sliced through the liver. The buck covered an estimated 300 yards before going down in the swamp. Mike had to don hip boots to trail the buck through water.

The buck's antlers had an inside spread of 19 6/8 inches and the longest tine measured 11 inches. Beams were 26 and 27 inches long. The carcass had a dressed weight of 202 pounds. During the week and a half between the time Mike first saw the book buck and he got it, he had another chance at a 4 or 6-pointer that he passed up. It's a good thing he did because that buck would have ended his hunt and he would have missed out on a chance at the booner.

The fact that most bowhunters are satisfied with any buck, if not any deer, is probably why so few B&C qualifiers have been tagged by archers. They frequently settle for the first deer that gives them a good shot. Serious trophy buck hunters must learn to pass up small bucks as Mike did, if they are to succeed.

Bill E. Smith, Jr. of Marquette with Boone and Crockett nontypical he dropped with a handgun in Marquette County during the 1991 firearms season.

Chapter 10

Handgun Hunts To Remember

Bill E. Smith, Jr. from Marquette didn't set out to be the first person to be recognized for bagging a Boone and Crockett (B&C) buck with a handgun in the state. It just turned out that way.

By the same token, Bill's son Mark, also of Marquette, didn't plan on bagging a pair of trophy 10-point bucks during the 1991 gun deer season, but that's what happened. Mark's biggest 10-pointer and his dad's best buck ever were dropped within minutes of each other and not very far apart. I think it's safe to say the father and son team were a pair of the state's happiest deer hunters after the 1991 gun season ended.

Bill also bagged a second buck, which was taken with his .44 magnum Ruger Redhawk revolver. He got a 6-pointer on opening day of firearm season, which was the first whitetail he took with a handgun. The booner was his second buck for the season and that whitetail alone would have been enough to make the Smiths' hunt a major success.

The huge nontypical rack has 18 scorable points, with the four longest tines measuring between 11 2/8 and 13 inches in length. One of the nontypical points on the right beam is a drop tine. Another drop tine that had been on the left antler was broken off. The rack's 8 nontypical points total over 30 inches in length.

The beams themselves were 27 7/8 and 27 inches long and the inside spread was 20 7/8 inches. The antlers had a final net score of 210 2/8. The rack ranks 15th among nontypicals in alltime records, according to the 3rd edition of <u>Michigan Big Game Records</u> and was a state record among nontypical handgun kills at the time it was taken. CBM started recognizing bucks bagged with handguns separately from other gun kills during 1990 and there were no nontypical entries through the

1990 scoring period.

The current state record nontypical taken with a handgun is a 21-pointer scoring 218 1/8 that the late Carl Mattson shot in Iron County during 1945. That head surfaced during 1993 even though the deer it was from was taken long before state records were being kept. The huge antlers from Smith's handgun buck remain as the largest nontypical on record for Marquette County.

The handgun Bill shot both of his bucks with during 1991 was a gift from some appreciative folks who he had done a lot of work for, remodeling their camp. At the time he received the gift, Smith promised the people he got it from that he would get a deer with it and he certainly came through on that promise. Bill said he had practiced with the Ruger a lot since he got it in 1987, but the fall of 1991 was the first time he hunted deer with it.

Bill has hunted whitetails in the U.P. throughout his life, starting when he was 14 years old. He was 53 when he scored on the big buck. Most of his hunting has been in Marquette County, but he said he's also shot deer in Menominee and Ontonagon Counties. He got his first buck near Marquette when 14 or 15 years old.

"I shot the 6-pointer with a double barreled 10 gauge shotgun that I borrowed from a friend," Bill recalled. "I remember both barrels going off, knocking me off the stump I was on, but I got the deer."

Many more bucks have fallen before him since then, including a pair of 10-points and a number of 8s. The 10s weren't as big as either of the bucks Mark got during '91. Most of Bill's deer hunting has been done with a rifle and he has been carrying a .30-06 during recent years. Smith has taken some does, too, mostly in Menominee County, including a pair of antlerless deer bagged with bow and arrow.

Smith comes from a long line of deer hunters. He said his father hunted whitetails until he was 80 years old. Mark is now carrying on the tradition, too, starting to hunt deer at 14, like his father did. The fall of 1991 was his 12th season. Mark said he didn't tag a deer during his first two or three years of hunting, then got a string of four does. He got his first buck, a spikehorn, during 1985. Since then he had taken two more bucks and some does before enjoying his best success ever during 1991.

Mark has been using a .280 Remington while deer hunting since 1989. He carried a .30-30 before getting the .280.

Like many other Michigan deer hunters, Bill and Mark don't hunt specifically for trophy bucks. They like to take a buck, any buck, when they can. They also understand the value of harvesting antlerless deer and do so when the opportunity presents itself. The pair also take advantage of the opportunity to shoot big bucks when they can, as they did in '91.

The Smiths got all four of their bucks during 1991 on a Marquette County mountain where few other hunters go. Mark's blind is about three-fourths of the way up the mountain and Bill posts on top. Bill said there are a lot of oak trees on the mountain, but they didn't produce any acorns during 1991. The father and son put bait out to increase their chances of seeing deer.

That fall was the second year the pair hunted the mountain. Mark got a 5-pointer from his blind during 1990 and also missed a big buck. He said the one he missed might be the larger of the two 10-pointers he got during 1991, but he said that buck's rack may have had more points. He doesn't think its rack was as big as the one his father got.

"The big buck I missed during 1990 caught me by surprise," Mark said. "There were two does in front of me and another deer was off in the distance that I thought was a buck, but it turned out to be another doe. Suddenly, the big buck came charging out from behind a tree at the does in front of me. He was running off by the time I got my rifle up and I missed him cleanly."

Bill saw a couple of big bucks from his blind during 1990, but not well enough to be able to get a shot at them. Based on their experiences that year, the pair made some adjustments near their blinds prior to their next hunt to increase their chances of getting any bucks they saw. The preparation obviously paid off. While hauling bait to their blinds toward the end of October, they saw where a pair of bucks fought on a skid trail.

"The ground was all tore up," Mark remembered.

"There were hundreds of tracks in the area," Bill commented. "You could see where a deer fell and the bucks pushed each other around."

The Smiths already knew big bucks were in the area based on what they saw during 1990. The scene of the fight confirmed the big boys were still there. The pair were full of anticipation as opening day of gun season approached.

Bill started off their successful season by shooting the 6-pointer with his revolver from his blind at 10:00 a.m. A team effort was required to recover that buck. Despite a solid hit, the whitetail covered some ground before going down. There was snow on the ground, so Bill and Mark were able to follow the deer easily, until it started wading a river. They had to walk the bank until they found where the whitetail left the river and the buck barely made it out of the water before going down.

It was Mark's turn to score on the morning of November 16th. At 9:00 a.m. a buck came into view with his nose to the ground, trailing a doe that had been at the bait. A well placed shot from the .280 killed that deer instantly. The 10-pointer was Mark's biggest deer ever, both in terms of antler and body size, and he was understandably pleased.

The buck had a dressed weight of 180 pounds and its age was estimated at 3 1/2. Bill's 6-point was 1 1/2 years old and the antlers were in keeping with a buck of that age. They took time out from hunting to have the two deer processed, then returned to their mountain blinds a couple of days later.

A warm front had moved in by then and began melting the snow that had been on the ground. Most of the snow was gone by Thursday, November 21st and that's the day Mark saw another buck. With most of the snow gone, it was harder to see deer because they blended with their surroundings. It was also harder to hear deer coming. Deer made noise as they walked in the crusted snow, but they made little, if any, noise while moving across the carpet of moisture-softened leaves that were present by the end of the first week of gun season.

It was late in the day when the buck appeared suddenly. The light was fading and the buck was running. Mark made out a 4 or 6-point rack on the deer's head, aimed as best as he could, then shot. He thought his sights were on the whitetail when he fired, but the bullet missed. Bill assisted Mark in scouring the area for sign of a hit or the buck and they found nothing.

Mark was disappointed at the time. After all, he had never filled two bucks tags in a season before. That was his first chance to do it and he missed. He couldn't know it at the time, but missing that buck was the best thing that could have happened. It set he and his father up for bagging the best bucks of their lives.

Conditions on November 22nd were similar to what they had been the day before. The temperature was above freezing and the leaves covering the ground were wet from melting snow and light rain that had fallen - ideal deer hunting conditions. The Smiths were back in their blinds during the morning. They made plans to sit until 10:00 a.m., at which time Bill was supposed to walk down hill to his son's blind.

Bill was on his way toward Mark at the appointed time when he heard his son shoot twice then begin hollering. When Bill reached Mark, he saw there was good reason for the hollering. Mark was standing over a buck bigger than either of them had ever taken. The 10-point antlers were huge and so was the deer. It was obviously a much better 10 than the one he got earlier in the season and Mark was elated.

Like the buck he missed the evening before, the big one appeared suddenly and was running. This time his aim was better. The first shot was on the money, but the buck was still on his feet, so Mark wasn't taking any chances. It didn't take long to get a second shell in the chamber with the pump action rifle. The whitetail went down as he fired the second time.

Mark is convinced his father chased the buck to him as Bill approached his blind. After congratulating his son and admiring the big buck, Bill left Mark to field dress the deer while he did some stillhunting. Conditions were ideal for noiselessly sneaking through the woods in search of whitetails. Bill said he likes to stillhunt as much as he does sitting in a blind. He routinely sits for a while in the morning then

Bill and Mark Smith with trophy bucks they bagged minutes apart.

pussyfoots around until 2:30 or 3:00 p.m., when he returns to his blind.

Bill was about 300 yards from Mark's blind when he saw a huge set of antlers turning 40 to 50 yards away.

"I didn't have any trouble seeing those horns," he said. "The buck stood up from his bed facing away from me. He must have heard a noise and didn't know where it came from."

As Bill grabbed the Ruger and cocked it, the huge buck turned broadside, giving the hunter a perfect target. Smith squeezed the trigger after taking careful aim and the buck dropped back in its bed. Bill hustled up to the fallen whitetail, ready for a second shot if one was needed, but the buck was dead.

Only about 20 minutes elapsed between the time Mark shot the big 10-pointer and Bill collected the massive nontypical. That's almost more good fortune than a pair of hunters can handle in such a short period of time, but the Smiths managed. If they felt good after Mark filled his second tag, they were as close to euphoric as deer hunters can get after Bill filled his.

The pair had no idea a buck with antlers of that size was any where near where they were hunting. Thinking back, Bill said he might have seen that deer from his blind the evening before he shot it. Shooting light had faded and he was getting ready to leave his blind when a big-bodied whitetail appeared. He said he thought it had to be a buck based on its size, but it was too dark to see antlers.

Interestingly, the B&C buck only had one good eye. The right eye had recently been injured, perhaps in a fight with another buck. The damage appeared to be too fresh to have happened during the buck fight the pair saw signs of during late October. As a result of the loss of an eye, that buck may not have survived through the upcoming winter, if Bill hadn't shot it.

The buck was extremely old. Its teeth were badly worn and estimates of the deer's age range between 8 1/2 and 11 1/2. Mark's second 10-pointer was aged at 5 1/2. That buck's antlers scored 141 7/8, also qualifying for a place in state records.

Although Bill's buck had the biggest rack, Mark's was the heaviest. It tipped the scales at 191 pounds versus 182 for Bill's. There was hardly any fat on the booner and the ribs on both sides were badly bruised, additional signs the old buck had been in a serious fight and might not have survived the winter.

I would sure like to see the buck that beat up on that big boy. So would Bill and Mark. Who knows. Maybe they will see him some day!

Coincidentally, a second B&C buck was taken with a handgun during the 1991 gun season. Even more amazing is the fact that both book bucks fell to handguns on the same day and each exceptional whitetail had a nontypical rack. As mentioned earlier, Bill Smith got his booner during the morning of November 22nd. Mark Janousek of Olivet nailed an impressive 25-pointer while hunting from a blind in Eaton County about 5:10 p.m. that day.

Janousek also used a .44 magnum revolver, but a Dan Wesson model with a 10-inch barrel. Mark's handgun was loaded with 300 grain XTP Hornady hollow point bullets that he handloaded. Smith used 240 grain semi-jacketed hollow point bullets in factory loads. Janousek's revolver was mounted with a two power scope and Smith used iron sights.

Antlers from the buck Mark shot with his revolver scored 203 7/8, despite the fact the rack had more points than the U.P. buck shot by Smith. Janousek's buck was also younger and smaller-bodied, but was still a terrific trophy. Mark's book buck was 4 1/2 and had a dressed weight of 158 pounds.

At 31 years of age in 1991, Mark Janousek hadn't had as much deer hunting experience as Bill Smith, but he had been very successful during the years he hunted. He had about 25 whitetails to his credit with gun and bow from Eaton and Calhoun Counties at the time. He had a lot more experience hunting deer with a handgun than Bill though. The B&C buck he got in 1991 was the 7th deer he had taken with his revolver.

Mark said he bought the used gun years earlier and first hunted deer with it the year handgun hunting was legalized in southern Michigan. He missed a nice 8-pointer with the gun that year, so didn't hunt with it for the next couple of years, but he continued practicing

Mark Janousek with nontypical booner he bagged on the same day the Smiths scored. (Photos courtesy Mark Janousek)

with the revolver to improve his accuracy. He was obviously better prepared when he resumed hunting with the .44 magnum because he hadn't missed with it since.

"I really like hunting with a handgun," Janousek said. "It's more accurate than my shotgun, if I have a rest. I shoot 3 1/2-inch groups at 100 yards with it, but when hunting I like to keep shots under 60 yards."

Mark said he normally hunts from a blind and frequently uses the blind's window sill as a rest for his scoped handgun. Due to the loud noise his gun makes when he shoots, he always carries ear plugs in his pockets and puts the foam rubber plugs in his ears before taking a shot at a deer. The plugs reduce the chances he will flinch in anticipation of the loud bang.

Like Bill, Mark's booner was the second buck he got with his handgun during 1991. At 8:15 a.m. on opening day of gun season, Mark bagged a nice 8-pointer with a 15 yard shot. The antlers had a 17 1/2-inch outside spread and he guessed the rack would score about 110. He had taken another buck or two with similar antlers.

Mark shot the 8-pointer from a different blind than the one where he got the large nontypical. He said his father saw the book buck one night during October along the edge of a wet swamp in the headlights of his car. Mark then put corn along the edge of the swamp and started hunting the area with his bow. The only buck he saw while bowhunting was a one-antlered spike and he passed it up.

On the third day of gun season, Mark passed up a 6-point that he watched breed a doe. On the 21st, he saw a big buck he would have shot, but it was too far away. He said he later found out that buck had 12-point antlers after a neighbor got the deer.

Janousek said he decided to give the swamp blind another try on the 22nd. He hadn't forgotten about the big-antlered deer his father saw. He said he wasn't real optimistic about seeing the buck, but knew there was a chance it could happen, and it did that evening.

Mark said the buck was 70 yards away when he first saw it. The whitetail was walking through water toward high ground at the edge of the swamp. It was obvious it was the same deer his father had seen because the antlers were huge with tines growing every where.

As the buck approached, Mark got excited, which is understandable under the circumstances. He fumbled around in his pockets for his ear plugs and couldn't find them. Rather than spend more time looking for the plugs, he substituted a pair of .44 shells and had them sticking out of ears when the buck stopped angling toward him at 23 paces.

The whitetail wheeled and ran at the shot, but only made it 70 or 80 yards before going down. It's amazing that two bucks of that caliber would fall to handguns in Michigan on the same day. This proves, once again, that you never know what's going to happen when deer hunting, which helps make each day afield a new adventure.

Michigan's first B&C buck with typical antlers in the handgun category, according to CBM records, was collected during the 1992 gun season by David Bastion in Genesee County. The Flushing resident got a 10-pointer scoring 172 1/8, Genesee County's highest scoring typical, on November 17th. Bastion said he saw the booner as he drove home from work that morning. The whitetail was about 400 yards from his house.

Once David got home, he didn't waste any time getting ready to try for the buck. He grabbed his Ruger .357 magnum handgun rather than his shotgun because he said it was more convenient to get quickly.

Although Bastion had not taken a whitetail with the revolver prior to 1992, he had claimed a mule deer with it while hunting out west and was confident in his shooting ability with the sidearm. He said he consistently hits a pie plate at 100 yards with the handgun, which is mounted with a 4X Tasco scope. As it turned out, long range accuracy wasn't necessary.

David was walking along a ditch paralleling a fence line toward where the buck had been when he spotted it 20 feet away on the opposite side of the fence row. The book buck was dropped with a 160 grain hollow point bullet from the pistol. At the rate booners are being bagged with handguns during the 1990s, it probably won't be long before another one is recorded.

Dave Bastion with Michigan's first Boone and Crockett typical taken with a handgun. (Photo courtesy Dave Bastion)

Red Friedrich with his 12-point nontypical that he bagged with a muzzleloader after missing it with a centerfire rifle during gun season.

Chapter 11

Second Chance Trophy

Red Friedrich of Shingleton is like most whitetail hunters across Michigan. He's primarily a meat hunter, but he's often dreamed of bagging a buck with a huge set of antlers. That dream came true during the December muzzleloader season in 1991.

Friedrich's big buck success was a matter of persistence and fate. The day Red got the trophy buck was actually the second chance he had at the deer. The whitetail got away the first time he saw it, but by continuing to hunt the same area, he eventually saw the buck again and scored.

If it weren't for fate, Red's hunt could have ended before he saw the big buck the first time. He saw a smaller buck one day that he almost got. If he had been successful in collecting that yearling whitetail then or on another day, his second and last buck tag would have been filled and the big buck's fate probably would have been different.

The fact that Red is a two season hunter also played an important role in his trophy buck success. He first saw the deer during the regular gun season. If Friedrich had failed to take advantage of additional hunting time offered by the special late season black powder hunt, he obviously wouldn't have tagged the buck of a lifetime.

At 35 years of age, Red had been hunting whitetails for almost 20 years and he bagged about 15 deer, six of which were antlered bucks. Antlered bucks are the only fair game in the northern U.P. where he lives, but he used to reside in the southern part of the state where he collected most of the does to his credit. He hunts primarily with a centerfire rifle, but he did take one doe with bow and arrow and hasn't bowhunted since then. The trophy buck was his first black powder kill.

Red is a self employed cabinet maker and his wife Carol is a professional quilting artist. They produce and sell North Woods Snowflakes, which are popular novelty items. The area where they live gets an abundance of snow every winter.

The Friedrichs live in a rural setting where they have electricity, but no running water. They get their water from a hand pump in their back yard. Since there are plenty of woods nearby, they do most of their deer hunting close to home.

Due to the presence of mature forests and long, cold winters, whitetails are not abundant where the Friedrichs live. However, hunting pressure is also light, which allows some bucks to reach ages at which they produce quality racks. Deer hunting from baited stands is the technique Red often relies on to increase his chances of seeing whitetails. Apples are his primary bait, but he also uses other foods such as cabbage.

The spot where Red shot the big buck is about a mile walk from where he parks his vehicle, so he normally only carries a small amount of bait with him each time he visits the stand. His ground blind is located in thick cover consisting of balsam fir and hemlock trees near an area that has been logged. The blind is near the southwest corner of the area that was cut over, where wild cherry trees and berry bushes are growing profusely. A large cedar swamp is not far from the stand site to the south and west.

The habitat is so thick that Red put bait 25 yards from his blind. The blind is constructed primarily of natural materials such as logs, limbs and evergreen boughs. An opening to shoot through is in the front of the structure. Deer that approach from the sides can be seen, but there's no opportunity to shoot in those directions.

The trophy buck Red bagged with a muzzleloader was actually the third deer he got from that blind and the second mature buck. The first year he hunted the spot he got a 3 1/2-year-old 9-pointer. That was the only whitetail Friedrich saw while hunting that year, which indicates how tough it can be to see deer in the country where he lives.

There had been a number of scrapes and antler rubbed trees near the blind that first year. One of the rubs was on a huge maple tree and Red thought a buck with a bigger rack than the one he got was responsible for that rub. Although the 9-pointer's antlers were respectable and would make most whitetail hunters happy, they scored about 100.

Gun tags that are not filled during the November firearm season remain valid during the December black powder hunt. Red purchased a second license after getting the 9-pointer. When he hadn't scored on a second buck by the end of November, he decided to try hunting with a muzzleloader. That year was the first time he hunted with a front loading rifle. He bought a Tompson/Center Scout in .50 caliber. His late season efforts went unrewarded that year. He didn't see a single deer while hunting.

Big buck sign didn't reappear near the blind where Friedrich got the 9-pointer the next fall, but he started putting bait there the week before gun season anyway. He had seen five bucks at other spots, two of which had been sighted in the area he decided to hunt on opening day. However, Red failed to see any deer from the new spot that day.

On the second day of the season he returned to the blind near the cutting where he had gotten the 9-pointer and was rewarded with another buck. This one was a forkhorn that fell to a well placed bullet from his .300 Savage.

"One deer is enough for Carol and I," Red said, "but I bought a second tag after I got the forkhorn to try to get some venison for a friend of mine. He had gotten a bear earlier in the fall and he didn't want the meat, so he gave it to us. I told him if I got another deer I would give the venison to him. The only reason I kept on hunting was to get some meat for my buddy."

And he almost got the venison he wanted one afternoon during the middle of gun season. As he approached the blind, he caught a glimpse of a deer feeding in front of it. The whitetail was a buck with another set of 4-point antlers and it was unaware of his presence.

There was about five inches of snow on the ground at the time, which helped cushion his foot steps, enabling him to sneak up on the buck. A white coating of snow sticking to trees at the site also made the buck easy to see. He stood out against the light background.

"I was carrying a thermos bottle and binoculars in my hands and had my rifle sling over my shoulder," Red related. "I put the stuff down as quietly as I could, got the rifle off my shoulder and was chambering a round when the buck simply walked off. He wasn't spooked, but he may have heard something he didn't like. The cover was so thick, he was gone before I could get a shot.

"If I would have gotten that buck, my hunt would have been over. If my rifle would have been in my hands instead of the other things, I would have shot that buck."

That goes to show what an important role fate can play in deer hunting. If Red had successfully bagged that second forkhorn, he probably would have been pleased. He would have secured a supply of venison for his friend and he wouldn't have had to endure subfreezing temperatures in his blind for several hours. However, he also would not have seen his best buck ever, the kind most hunters can only dream about. If events of that day had been just a little different, Red may never have known such a buck existed.

Although Red couldn't realize it at the time, it was fortunate he didn't get that second forkhorn. Once the buck was out of sight, he slipped into his blind as quickly and quietly as possible. He thought the yearling might return.

It didn't, but a pair of does were feeding in front of the blind about 5:00 p.m. when they suddenly took off running. Earlier that season, a friend of Red's grunted when he had some skiddish does in front of him and a big 8-pointer came running in to investigate. The hunter promptly shot the buck and put his tag on it.

Remembering his friend's experience, Red decided to try grunting, too. He didn't have a call, but did the best he could to imitate a pig-like grunt with his voice. To his surprise, the does came back, but they were only in view briefly before moving off again. So Red grunted a second time.

Light snow was falling as Friedrich saw a deer approaching once more. It was coming from the direction the does had gone, so he thought they were coming back. Then the whitetail abruptly lifted its head, along with a huge set of antlers.

"I was thinking, 'Holy cow, what do I do now,' when I realized it was a big buck," Red said. "My rifle was leaning against the blind because I was caught totally off guard. I thought the buck was a doe.

"Because of the thick balsams, I could only see the buck's head. He threw his head back and sniffed the air as I reached for my rifle. When he didn't see or smell anything he started walking and his body was screened by balsams the whole time.

"By the time I got the rifle up he was almost out of the area where I could shoot, so I took the only shot I thought I had, aiming at his head. When I shot, the muzzle blast knocked snow off the front of the blind, blocking my view. I still felt confident I got him and he would be laying where I last saw him.

"Boy, was I in for a disappointment. There was no blood or hair or nothing. There were so many tracks in the snow that I had a hard time telling which ones were his. I looked all around and didn't find any sign that I hit him.

"I had a pretty sick feeling when I got home that evening. Missing a big buck is one of the worst feelings in the world. I kept wondering what I had done wrong or that maybe I hadn't looked around enough. I had to double check the next day. Needless to say, I didn't get much sleep that night.

"It happened so quick that I didn't know how many points he had. I just knew he was big. The rack was also tall. The antlers were real high."

The following day, Red didn't find anything new. It was obvious that he had missed the buck. If his bullet had connected, the buck would have been dead in his tracks. Nonetheless, he hunted the blind during the remainder of gun season, keeping a watchful eye for ravens. If the buck was down, the scavenging birds would surely find it and lead him to the carcass by their calls.

Red saw no feeding ravens and he also saw no more deer. The size of that buck's antlers haunted him during the remainder of gun season and he kept thinking about it as muzzleloader season approached. Opening day was December 6th. He had no idea how the rack would rate scorewise. All he knew was that the antlers were the biggest he had ever seen on a whitetail in the wild. Despite the fact he knew the chances of seeing that same buck again were not high, he hoped he would.

That's why he kept putting bait at the spot where he missed the big boy. The food was eaten regularly, so he figured he would at least see some whitetails even if he didn't see the big one. Red knew another forkhorn was in the area. Perhaps he would see that buck again.

Red's absence in the blind overlooking the bait during the week between the end of gun season and the beginning of the black powder hunt probably helped. Local deer may have relaxed some during the week the blind remained vacant. The food source may have also become more attractive to whitetails by the time muzzleloader season opened as the weather turned colder and more snow accumulated on the ground.

By the time black powder season opened, a total of 24 inches of snow had fallen. Red said he and Carol keep a running total of snowfall on their calendar. Half of that total accumulated during the two days preceding the opener. Ten inches fell on the 4th of December and two inches came down on the 5th.

Temperatures were in the 20s when Red hiked to his remote blind on the afternoon of the 6th. He was starting to get cold by 5:00 p.m. when he saw movement off to the right. A doe and her two youngsters ran toward the blind and started feeding. Soon after the deer arrived, the doe stood up on her hind legs, looking back the way they had come from. She obviously heard something coming and Red followed her example in an effort to find out what it was.

It was the big buck that had occupied so many of Friedrich's thoughts over the past two weeks.

"He marched right in toward the does," Red said. "I had time to get the gun up as he approached. I picked out an opening to shoot through and when he reached the opening he stopped perfectly. Then I prayed the gun would go off, and it did."

Hit through the lungs with a round ball, the trophy whitetail stumbled back the way it had come, but didn't get far before dropping.

"By the time he was down, I was shaking pretty good," Red remembered. "I was going to reload, but I got too excited and went to look at him. When I reached the deer, the right antler was the only one visible and it had four long points, so I thought it was a big 8-pointer."

When Red lifted the left antler out of the snow, he was in for a real surprise. It didn't match the right beam at all, having twice as many points. There were four nontypical points, including one that was 16 1/8 inches long. It was almost like a third beam.

"When I pulled my knife out to gut the deer I realized my hands were cold. Rather than take a chance of cutting myself, I decided to get help."

Another hunter who Red knows parked near Red's vehicle that day and was waiting for him when he reached the road. He had heard the shot. Red had told the guy about the big buck he had missed during November and he doubted his description of the rack, so Red decided to have fun with him.

Antlered bucks must have spikes that are at least three inches long to be legal. Red told the guy he got a buck that was "barely legal" in terms of antler size and asked for his help to drag the deer to the road. The other hunter agreed to help, but he was anxious to get the job done quickly because his wife would have his dinner waiting for him.

"When he saw that buck, he forgot about dinner," Red laughed. "There was a lot of hooping and hollering in the woods that night."

Red's 12-point nontypical had a net score of 181 3/8 and was the highest scoring buck bagged with a muzzleloader that year. It ranks fourth in state records among nontypical black powder kills. The fact that all of the nontypical tines were on the left side indicates the buck may have had an injury of some type on his right side at one time.

The nontypical tines weren't the only ones that were long on the rack. The longest typical tine taped 14 6/8 inches. Although the rack was tall, it wasn't real wide. The inside spread was 16 7/8 inches. The buck was 6 1/2 years old and had a dressed weight of 170 pounds.

Red did give venison from the buck to the friend he got the bear meat from. Although primarily a meat hunter, Friedrich was happy to get the antlers grown by that unique U.P. buck, even though it took him two chances to finally connect.

Red Friedrich with his 12-point nontypical that he bagged with a muzzleloader after missing it with a centerfire rifle during gun season.

Matt Usitalo with Houghton County's best typical, which was taken during the 1992 gun season.

Chapter 12

Houghton County's Best

If Matt Usitalo of Houghton was superstitious, he probably isn't anymore. For those who are superstitious, the number 13 is considered bad luck and the fall of 1992 was Usitalo's 13th year of deer hunting. Matt not only had the good fortune of bagging a big buck, he got one with the largest typical rack known taken by a hunter in the state that year.

The massive 10-point antlers from Houghton County had a gross score of 187 and a final official net score after deductions of 179 5/8, ranking the rack as the second largest typical on record for the U.P. and seventh for the state, according to Commemorative Bucks of Michigan (CBM), the state's big game record keeper. Matt's buck is actually tied for second and seventh places respectively with a 12-pointer that scored exactly the same and that was bagged in Iron County during 1927 by the late John Schmidt. Another 12-pointer taken in Baraga County during 1987 by Louis Roy from L'anse, covered elsewhere in this book, is the U.P.'s highest scoring typical at 184 7/8.

Besides being the highest scoring typical known taken in Michigan during the 1992 season, it's the best typical on record for Houghton County.

Usitalo's buck apparently led a charmed life until it crossed his path on the third evening of the 1992 gun season because a number of local hunters reported seeing and taking shots at the unmistakable whitetail after Matt tagged it. One hunter told Usitalo that a bullet he fired at the buck grazed the animal during the fall of 1991. Matt's younger brother Mike also missed what he feels is the same deer during November of 1991.

It was the fifth day of gun season when Mike saw the exceptional buck standing in an area that had been logged a couple of years before. The animal was surrounded by thick saplings that had sprouted, but Mike thought he could find an opening in the brush for one of his bullets. He had seven shells for his rifle and he fired every one of them while the whitetail stood his ground and the trophy whitetail remained motionless after he emptied his rifle, apparently unaware of where the shots were coming from.

The saplings obviously deflected all of Mike's shots and he was so intent on the deer that he was out of shells before he had the chance to anticipate that happening. He was convinced one of his bullets would connect, until they were all gone. Imagine the excitement, frustration and panic involved in being so close to the buck of a lifetime and not being able to do anything about it!

After exhausting his supply of ammunition Mike rushed home, grabbed Matt's rifle, along with shells for it, and raced back to the spot where the buck had been, hoping it might still be there. It was gone by then, of course. Matt said the buck was 6 1/2 years old when he got it and its rack was similar the year before. That statement is not only based on Mike's description of the deer. Matt saw the buck himself during the fall of 1991, too, but not while hunting.

The evening before Mike missed the whitetail, Matt saw it in the headlights of his vehicle as it crossed the road ahead of him. It was headed toward the clearcut where his brother would see it the next day. The big deer didn't stay in the clearcut though because when Matt drove by the same area 1 1/2 hours later, he saw the buck cross the road again, going in the opposite direction.

It's no secret that bucks are extremely active during November as they become preoccupied with the rut. When they aren't with an estrus doe, they are looking for one, constantly checking scrapes and the breeding condition of local does. The book buck was probably doing just that when he was seen by Matt and Mike and who knows how many other hunters during the fall of '91. The deer obviously crossed the paved road where Matt saw him, numerous times. He had to cross the road at least one more time in less than 24 hours before Mike saw him.

Although the fall of 1992 was Matt's 13th year of deer hunting, the booner he bagged was only the second whitetail he had ever shot. He tagged his first deer, a small 8-pointer, the previous fall and luck played a major role in his getting that one. He was on his way to put some apples out for bait in his vehicle when a deer crossed the road ahead of him and stopped in a field. Matt said he thought he saw antlers on the deer's head, so he parked his vehicle, got out with his rifle and took a better look through his scope.

After confirming the whitetail was a buck, as it remained standing in the field, Matt took careful aim and dropped it instantly with a head shot. After shooting the deer, he realized he didn't have a knife with him to field dress it with, so he returned home. He had only been gone about 10 minutes.

"What do you need," his parents asked him as he walked in the door.

"A knife to gut the buck I got," was his reply.

"Ya, sure," they chuckled, positive that he was kidding.

"That 8-pointer was the first buck I had a good shot at," Matt said. "I have seen others over the years, but I either didn't see them long enough to get a shot or they were running. Something always seemed to happen to cause a poor shot or no shot at all when ever I saw a buck."

Matt remembers getting shots at four bucks during his first 10 years of hunting, including a big nontypical and a "decent 8-pointer" in Ontonagon County. In each case, his bullets missed their mark. He was always confident that if he could get a good shot at a standing buck, he would score and the 8-pointer during 1991 proved him right. Although that buck had a rack, it was only 1 1/2 years old.

Even though Matt knew a trophy buck was in the area based on his and Mike's experiences during 1991, he never really thought about trying for that deer. As an average deer hunter, he is content to collect any buck. Besides, he didn't think he had a chance of bagging a Boone and Crockett class buck.

He had seen a 6-pointer in a field near his home and an 8-pointer while bowhunting. Those were the bucks that were on Matt's mind when he decided to post behind the house after dinner on the evening of November 17th. He had an apple pile there that some deer were visiting. There was less than a hour of shooting light remaining in the day anyway, so there wasn't time to go anywhere else.

Usitalo had been in position for about 20 minutes when he heard a noise that he thought was made by a deer, so he got ready. About 30 seconds later he heard another noise. Then he caught movement out of the corner of his eye as a whitetail emerged from behind a couple of evergreen trees 35 to 40 yards away.

The antlers were obvious. The buck walked about 15 feet into the open and stopped.

"That buck had no intention of going to the bait pile," Matt said. "He was walking off to the side. I let the shot go as soon as I could before it changed its mind and took off."

Matt was hunting with a lever action .30-30 rifle loaded with 170 grain bullets. The rifle was mounted with a 3X-9X power scope and he said he had the scope on 5X or 6X when he took the shot. Although well hit, the buck ran 30 to 50 yards before going down.

"I knew the buck had a large rack, but I didn't know really how big it was until I got to it," Matt said.

He was excited, surprised, impressed, elated and shocked all at once. He had so much adrenaline flowing that he pulled the carcass into the open from the thick cover where it died, all by himself. That was no small feat considering the deer probably weighed close to 300 pounds on the hoof. The dressed weight was 245 pounds.

Matt said that he had a hard time moving the carcass later after it had been field dressed and he had calmed down some, despite the fact it was lighter than when he initially moved it.

It's easy to understand why that buck generated so much excitement. Both beams are heavy and long. I took rough measurements of the antlers a few days after Matt got the buck and the smallest circumference was 4 3/8 inches. Antler bases were 5 1/2 inches around. The right beam was over 30 inches long and the left was almost as long. Some shrinkage obviously took place by the time the rack was officially scored because the right beam was 29 6/8 inches then and the left was 29.

At the time, the inside spread was 21 5/8 inches (it shrunk to 21 3/8) and the tines ranged between 6 2/8 and 10 inches in length. The antlers are truly impressive. The fact that bucks of that caliber still roam the U.P. should serve was encouragement for hunters who hope to bag a trophy buck like it some day. It's real encouraging in view of the fact that two of the highest scoring typical racks ever known to have been grown in the U.P. were documented during recent years. There are bound to be others like them in the U.P.'s vast forests some where.

Houghton County, for example, has always produced some quality bucks, but it seems to really be coming on strong during the 1990s. B&C qualifying bucks were bagged in the county during 1990 and 1991 as well as '92. Robert Marr from Calumet got a 15-point nontypical in the county during 1990 that scored 196 3/8. The minimum for nontypical B&C entries is 195. The buck that Marr got, incidentally, was his first.

County resident Michael McCloskey claimed a typical antlered booner during the 1991 gun season that scored 170 3/8. Typical racks must measure a minimum of 170 to qualify for B&C entry. McCloskey's buck was one of 20 from Houghton County that qualified for state records that fall, which was the highest tally for any county in the state that year.

Eight book bucks from the county had been listed in state records for 1992 besides Usitalo's. Although the number of entries was down from '91, the county still had a good showing of trophy bucks. Matt's buck alone keeps the county in the running as one of the U.P.'s best locations to try for trophy whitetails.

As far as Matt is concerned, the 1992 gun season was his best ever, despite the fact it was his 13th. His luck was all good and he wouldn't mind if the lucky streak continues in the future. However, it's going to be tough to beat the luck and the buck that came his way during 1992, no matter how many more years he hunts whitetails.

Robert Marr with a Boone and Crockett nontypical taken in Houghton County during 1990. It was Marr's first deer.

Top: Jerry Pennington of Oxford with his late season booner. He bow bagged the buck on December 22, 1992. Bottom: Pennington with 10-pointer he claimed with a bow and arrow during 1991 that just missed the Boone and Crockett minimum of 170. (Photos courtesy Jerry Pennington)

Chapter 13

Late Season Payoff

Jerry Pennington from Oxford made Michigan bowhunting history during December of 1992 when he arrowed an exceptional 10-point whitetail that had antlers large enough to qualify for national records maintained by the Boone and Crockett Club. That year marked the first time that bowhunters in the state managed to take two bucks of that caliber, according to state records maintained by CBM. Ron Visser from Ada tagged the first one during November. The 10-pointer measured 175 6/8.

Only seven B&C bucks had been bagged by archers in the state, including Pennington's, through 1992 seasons, so it's obvious whitetails with antlers of such gigantic proportions aren't collected by bowhunters every year. However, that may be changing. The fall of 1992 marked the third year in a row that booners were tagged by bowhunters.

What's even more amazing is the fact that 1991 was almost the first year that a pair of B&C qualifiers were collected by bowhunters and another big 10-pointer Pennington got was the one that would have done it. That buck had a final official score of 169 5/8, 3/8-of-an-inch shy of the magic 170 minimum required for typical antlers to qualify for B&C listing. The monster buck Jerry got during 1992 exceeded that mark, scoring 174 7/8.

Collecting two book bucks like that two years in a row is unprecedented in Michigan bowhunting records. What are the secrets that enabled Pennington to take those two bucks? He really doesn't have any secrets. His one-of-a-kind success is the result of lots of scouting to locate areas where big bucks live along with plenty of patience, persistence and will power to pass up smaller bucks until he gets a shot at the deer he wants. He practices a lot with bow and arrow, too, to increase the odds that he will connect on the buck he wants when the chance he has been waiting for finally arrives.

Other hunters who are willing and able to do the same things can follow in Jerry's foot steps. What is especially noteworthy about the trophy buck he collected in 1992 is the fact it was taken toward the end of hunting season on December 22nd. All of the big bucks obviously aren't shot during the November gun season and there are probably more of them that survive during years like 1992 when wet weather prevents farmers from harvesting their corn. Hunters who don't score during one season may be able to connect during the next. Those who are persistent like Jerry, don't give up hope as long as hunting season is open.

The fact that Pennington has taken a number of bucks that qualify for state records over the years with both bow and gun makes it easier for him to hold out for whitetails with the biggest racks that he can find. His tally over the three year period ending in '92 was absolutely phenomenal. The fall of 1990 was his best year in terms of quantity and quality when he tagged three bucks, all of which qualified for state records.

One of the bow-bagged bucks from 1990 was the highest scoring whitetail he had taken until then. It was a 16-point nontypical measuring 163 3/8. The other buck Jerry got with his bow was a typical 9-pointer taping 130 7/8.

The deer Pennington took with a shotgun that year ranks as the highest scoring buck he's claimed with firearms, but not by much. The 10-pointer tallied 140 4/8, 3/8-of-an-inch more than his previous best gun kill, another 10-point that fell to his shotgun in 1987.

The annual bag limit for bucks was four during 1990. Two could be taken with bow and arrow and two with firearms. That was the last year for such a liberal bag limit on bucks. The annual limit for antlered whitetails was reduced to two per year starting in 1991.

At any rate, two of the three book bucks Jerry got in 1990 were taken with archery equipment during October and the third fell to his shotgun during gun season. Jerry concentrated on even higher quality bucks in 1991 and '92. He arrowed the 10-pointer that just missed B&C minimums on opening day of the early bow season during 1991. Four days later, he had a chance to fill his second tag with another bruiser that had 18 points.

The buck was 35 to 40 yards away and he was with a group of five other whitetails. An 8-pointer was standing in front of the big one and a 6-pointer was behind him. The shot was further than Jerry likes to shoot and it was windy, but he felt it was the best chance he was going to have. The wind caught his arrow and he got the 8-pointer instead of the one he wanted.

The smaller whitetail proved to be a heck of a consolation prize. Its antlers scored 120 5/8. Most bowhunters would gladly settle for a buck of that caliber.

Then during October of 1992 Jerry's first buck was another one any deer hunter, not just archers, would be envious of. It was a 10-pointer scoring 153 6/8. He got it on the third morning of the early bow season when it walked by his tree stand broadside at a distance of 30 feet.

Jerry said he passed up a number of smaller bucks before getting that one. The experienced archer does so much preseason scouting that he normally has an excellent idea where his chances of ambushing a big buck are best when the season opens. If one spot doesn't pan out, he normally learns enough by watching whitetail movements from that position to choose a site that's better.

Pennington practices daily with his bow to hone his shooting skills. If he's doing well, he may only shoot a half dozen arrows at a time.

"If the first two arrows are on the money, I quit then," Jerry said. "Putting those first arrows where you want them helps build confidence. You're not going to get a second shot at a big buck, so you want that first arrow to count."

The bowhunter shoots a Martin Warthog bow and the draw weight is set just under 70 pounds. He shoots aluminum arrows tipped

Jerry with his first buck during 1992. The 10-pointer scored 153 6/8. (Photo courtesy Jerry Pennington)

with Thunderhead 125 broadheads. His bow is equipped with three sight pins. One is set for shots at deer right under him when in a tree stand, the second is on at 18 or 20 yards and the third is for 30 yard shots.

Jerry didn't get to bowhunt as much as he likes to during 1992 because he had started a new job and didn't have the time. When he has a day off he usually hunts from daylight until 11:00 a.m. during the morning, then 3:00 p.m. until dark. On days he works, he tries to hunt as long as he can in the evening.

The reason Pennington didn't fill his second buck tag during October or November in 1992, besides the fact he didn't hunt as much as usual, was that he didn't get a shot at another whitetail he wanted to take. Although Jerry had never shot a buck during December prior to 1992, he had done some hunting then and a lot of scouting. Even in years when he was done hunting during October, he often spent time scouting during December to keep track of deer movements and to try to determine how many bucks made it through gun season.

Based on that experience, Jerry knew that deer movements are often much different during December than the two previous months and that whitetails sometimes change areas. Nonetheless, he found hunting during the late season frustrating. He had more difficulty finding bucks than previous years. They changed habits more frequently, making them more unpredictable.

The fact that there was still a lot of standing corn contributed to the difficulty in pinpointing a good buck. A lot of them were staying in cornfields, at least during legal shooting hours. Buck activity was sporadic. Jerry said he would see eight antlered whitetails some days and maybe only one the next.

There was no fresh deer sign around the tree stands that had been so productive during October and November, so Pennington had to go elsewhere and try his luck from the ground. He finally settled on a little peninsula of high grass and weeds next to an 80 acre cornfield.

"This is a really great spot to kill a buck," Jerry thought when he found the spot. "But I never dreamed of killing a buck like the one I got from the ground. I was getting ready to settle for something else."

The weeds on the peninsula were high enough that they screened Jerry from view when sitting. Three rows of corn had been cut near the peninsula on December 21st. It was real windy that evening and Jerry didn't see a single deer. He figured they simply weren't moving and returned the next afternoon.

It was still windy and cold that day, but not as windy as it had been the day before. The air temperature was below freezing and the wind chill made it feel even colder. The book buck appeared along the edge of the cut corn during late afternoon. Other deer were already in the open feeding when he showed up.

"He came walking along the edge of the corn feeding like he didn't have a care in the world," Jerry said. "He looked smaller than he really was. I thought his rack might score in the 150s or 160s, but it didn't matter at the time. I knew he was a good buck and I was ready to take him if I could. I was really pumped up seeing him come out of the corn."

Jerry watched the book buck for about 10 minutes before he took his shot. He let him get within 10 yards before releasing an arrow. He had dropped to his knees as the buck approached and made the shot through an opening in the weeds.

Even when the archer walked up to the fallen whitetail, he didn't realize it was a booner. He said the rack didn't look balanced and he figured there would be a lot of deductions. A week later, Jerry measured the antlers and he came up with a figure in the 160s. He was surprised and elated when CBM measurer John Major from Troy discovered the rack exceeded 170 after the required drying period.

Jerry said the buck was 4 1/2 or 5 1/2 years old and dressed out at 180 pounds without a speck of fat on him. The buck had a broken nose and the cape was all scarred up from fighting. The cape was in such bad shape, Jerry's taxidermist used a different one to mount the deer.

Pennington wore a set of insulated brown coveralls for his late season hunt. He said the garment is warm and quiet. He's owned the coveralls since he started deer hunting many years ago and they've only been washed once. He puts all of his hunting clothes in plastic garbage bags when he's not wearing them to reduce the chances of them becoming contaminated with foreign odors.

Due to the bulkiness of the coveralls, Jerry wears an armguard to keep his bow string from hitting the material. The bowhunter always wears a head net, too, to eliminate glare from his glasses. He used to wear contact lenses, but prefers glasses.

Jerry said he passed up 15 to 20 bucks before getting his booner and he's certainly glad he did. Incidentally, that buck is the first B&C qualifier taken in Oakland County, according to CBM records. Passing up smaller bucks is essential if you're serious about getting a big one. So is being persistent, sticking it out as long as possible in an effort to succeed. Jerry's experience proves it!

The late Albert Tippett with Michigan's heaviest whitetail shot in Ontoagon County during 1919. The buck had an official dressed weight of 354 pounds and estimated live weight of 425 pounds.

Chapter 14

The State's Heavy Weights

The heaviest whitetail known taken in the state was a monster buck with a dressed weight of 354 pounds and an estimated live weight of 425 pounds. Flint resident Albert Tippett bagged the enormous buck near Trout Creek in Ontonagon County on the last day of the 1919 gun season. That deer had a 10 or 12-point rack that probably would have qualified for a place in state records, according to Tippett's son-in-law James Procunier of Ishpeming.

The problem is that no one knows where the rack is from Tippett's trophy. Procunier said the mounted head of that buck hung in a camp near Ishpeming owned by the late Ted Anderson on County Road 581 for many years, but the mount disappeared after Anderson's death. It sure would be nice to locate that set of antlers to find out how much they score.

The day Tippett shot the state's heaviest buck, he didn't start hunting until 11:30 a.m., according to Procunier. It was a Sunday and it had been snowing since the previous Tuesday. The accumulated snow was waist deep where it drifted. About 1:30 p.m., Tippett jumped the big buck from where it was bedded underneath a snow-covered spruce tree and dropped it with one shot when it paused after running 70 feet.

Whitetails with the second, third and fourth heaviest verified weights were also U. P. bucks and each of those animals had impressive antlers that were measured and are listed in state records. The late L. E. Valley, Sr. of Pinconning, for example, tagged a megabuck near Raco in Chippewa County during 1925 that pulled the railroad scales at Brimley to the 345 pound mark, according to his son. The exceptional

U.P. HALL OF FAME WHITETAILS

GROSS SCORE ___ 206 $\frac{7}{8}$

FINAL SCORE ___ 204 $\frac{1}{8}$

COUNTY TAKEN ___ **IRON**

COUNTY RANK ___ 6   TYP.   NON-TYP.   ✓

Mount of a buck with a dressed weight of 324 pounds that the late Leo Furaitor shot in Iron County during 1967.

buck was in the company of two other big bucks and four does when they were chased past his stand by a free-roaming dog. A nontypical rack graced the fallen buck's head that scores 203 5/8.

The 25-pointer ranks second among nontypicals in Chippewa County and 30th for the state, according to CBM records.

The next two heavy weights, both of which were bagged in Iron County, grew B&C racks, too. One had a typical rack and the other a nontypical. Interestingly, only one pound separates the weight of those two.

Amasa resident Leo Furaitor bagged a 13-point buck in 1967 that had a dressed weight of 324 pounds and a nontypical score of 204 1/8. That rack ranks 26th in alltime records and 6th for Iron County. That county produced a lot of big nontypicals over the years.

A dressed weight of 323 pounds was registered for the huge typical bagged by John Schmidt of Crystal Falls in 1927. Schmidt was a stander on a drive when he collected the 12-pointer, according to his son, and measurements of the antlers tallied 179 5/8. Horses were used to get Schmidt's big buck out of the woods. The antlers from that buck are the largest on record for Iron County, among typicals, are in the number two spot for the U.P. and in 7th place for the state.

There are four more Michigan bucks with known dressed weights that surpassed the 300-pound mark. The next heaviest also came from the U.P.'s Iron County. The late Dick Stoychoff bagged a 12-pointer with a dressed weight of 318 pounds on November 30, 1939.

The big buck was reportedly taken on a drive and a lucky shot from Stoychoff's 12 gauge shotgun dropped the whitetail. The shotgun was loaded with 00 buckshot and one of the pellets hit the buck behind an ear. The trophy deer was estimated to be nine years old and the antlers scored 164, putting them in 8th place among typicals for Iron County.

The late Art Basch bagged the next heaviest whitetail for the state in Leelanau County on November 15, 1943, according to wife Laura. That was the year the county reopened to deer hunting after a long closure.

The 11-point buck had a dressed weight of 317 pounds. Mrs. Basch said her husband was hunting on her brother's potato farm when he spotted the monster buck on a ridge. A well placed shot from a newly-acquired Remington .32 special dropped the deer.

While dragging the heavy buck to a nearby road, Mrs. Basch said her husband saw a second buck on the same ridge where he scored. She added that a third trophy class buck crossed his path while walking to where he parked his car.

The buck was weighed at a grocery store in Glen Arbor. The nontypical antlers scored an even 150. Art usually got a buck every year during hunting season until his death in 1965.

John Schmidt's grandson Jack looks at mount of an Iron County buck his grandfather shot in 1927 that had a dressed weight of 323 pounds.

Roland Johnson of Chatham with the state's heaviest bow kill, a 9-pointer that tipped the scales at 273 pounds after being field dressed.

Another 317 pound buck was killed by a car on October 22, 1980 in Washtenaw County, according to DNR Big Game Specialist Ed Langenau. The animal was 4 1/2 years old and its antlers scored 131 3/8. Langenau said Missaukee County yielded a 311-pounder to Ray Gould from Hopewell, Virginia in 1977.

The heaviest buck bagged by a bowhunter tipped the scales at 277 pounds, according to Langenau. He said the whitetail was taken in Allegan County during 1946. He added that the same county produced another huge buck for a bowhunter during 1942 that weighed in at 263 pounds.

The honor for the second largest buck bagged by a bowhunter, however, goes to Roland Johnson from Chatham. The veteran deer hunter arrowed a 9-point in Alger County on October 29, 1989 that had a dressed weight of 273 pounds.

Johnson was perched on the limbs of a cherry tree watching a runway leading to a field when the huge whitetail he bagged appeared at 5:55 p.m. He waited until the deer was 15 yards away before drawing his 50 pound pull compound bow and sending a carefully-aimed arrow into its chest cavity.

When Roland reached the fallen buck he marveled at the size of the animal's body and was also impressed with its large antlers. Even though he realized the buck was big, he underestimated its weight by

111

about 50 pounds. He guessed the carcass' field dressed weight at 225 pounds.

The experienced hunter knows what a 200-pound buck looks like because he tagged another heavy animal wearing an 8-point rack with a bow and arrow during the fall of 1987. That buck weighed 215 pounds. Ironically, the 8-pointer was also arrowed on October 29th.

Johnson had been bowhunting for 10 years and the huge 9-point was his 8th kill with archery equipment. He hunted every day of bow season during 1989 and saw two other bucks that were smaller, but neither of them were in position for a bow shot. The archer admitted he was considering shooting a doe when the big buck changed his mind.

Randy Westerfield from Constantine also bagged a big buck with bow and arrow during the 1989 season. He scored in St. Joseph County on October 6th, taking an 8-pointer that dressed out at 260 pounds. The buck was Randy's first whitetail. He was 18 years old at the time.

Randy said he was sitting at one end of a cornfield with his bow and arrows, waiting for deer to show, when the big-bodied buck appeared at the opposite end of the field and entered the corn. He snuck toward the buck, covering 250 to 300 yards before spotting the deer in an open pocket in the corn 20 to 25 yards away. The whitetail was uphill from Westerfield and his well placed arrow pierced the lungs before severing its spine, dropping the animal on the spot.

The buck's antlers had an inside spread over 20 inches and a score of 134. Roland's 9-point measured 130 6/8.

Little documentation of the weights of whitetail does has been attempted by hunters in Michigan. However, one of the heaviest, if not the heaviest, doe for the state was taken by Mark Ritchie from Dexter on his first deer hunt in 1969. The 14-year-old bagged a doe with a dressed weight of 240 pounds in Washtenaw County. Ritchie is best known for a buck he bagged in 1984 that presently ranks as the state record typical, according to CBM.

The late Art Basch with a Leelanau County giant that weighed 317 pounds dressed. (Photo courtesy Mrs. Art Basch)

Chippewa County buck called Bucky by those who knew him. He was 9 1/2 when this photo was taken. The old buck was taken by a hunter during December of 1984 when 10 1/2 years old.

Chapter 15

Michigan's Oldest Whitetails

The oldest buck on record for Michigan and perhaps for all of North America, was over 17 years old. That buck, which was named Pete, spent most of his years at the Hercules Powder Plant in Ishpeming. Area resident Edwin Rosewall, who was an employee at the plant, remembers old Pete.

Rosewall said one whitetail doe was trapped on the plant's premises when a fence was constructed around the facility. That doe gave birth to a pair of buck fawns in 1944, one of which was Pete.

The plant's owners and employees adopted the two bucks, feeding them lettuce and doughnuts to supplement browse they obtained on their own, according to Rosewall. The bucks moved around freely during winter months by following the same roads and paths used by employees.

Rosewall doesn't remember any specifics about the bucks' antlers, except they were big when the animals were in their prime. He said they grew their largest racks when they were between three and eight years of age. Rosewall said he regrets not making an effort to recover Pete's antlers when the buck shed them. If he would have, he could have had an entire collection of the buck's racks throughout its life.

As it was, the former Hercules employee only recovered one beam from one of Pete's last sets of antlers. That antler has four points on it.

Rosewall said both bucks weighed about 185 pounds all of their adult lives. Pete's brother was eventually killed by dogs at the plant, according to Rosewall. He said their mother may have met a similar fate, but he isn't sure exactly what happened to her. Pete's brother still lived longer than most bucks, being between 12 and 14 years old when killed.

Interestingly, Pete's brother was never given a name. In fact, Pete came by his name late in life after his brother was dead.

The Hercules plant closed in 1961, which was Pete's 17th year. At that time, personnel from the DNR's Cusino Wildlife Research Station at Shingleton caught Pete in a live trap and brought him to the state facility.

Former DNR Deer Researcher Louis Verme, who is now retired, also remembers Hercules Pete. Verme recalled that Pete had spike antlers still in velvet during the fall of 1961 when the buck was moved. Retention of velvet on the antlers indicated an imbalance in hormones.

Verme said they put Pete in a pen with another buck and Pete immediately started fighting with it, indicating he still had plenty of spunk. However, the old buck's days were numbered. He died that winter, his 18th, at Cusino. Pete was found dead in his pen one morning following a subzero night that was apparently too much for him.

In the wild, bucks seldom reach 10 years of age, but there are a few records of animals that have done so. A 7-pointer shot in west Delta County during the fall of 1988, for example, proved to be 12 1/2 years old. The buck was shot by Tim Gerou from Trout Lake after Thanksgiving.

Former DNR District Wildlife Biologist Dick Aartila at Escanaba said the buck is the oldest he had seen during 30 years of aging them. He aged the deer at 13 1/2 based on tooth wear and had a cross section of a tooth examined to verify the whitetail's age. The cross section verified the buck's age at 12 1/2.

The buck was Gerou's first whitetail. He had been hunting deer on and off for 10 years and that one was the first he saw antlers on and the first one he ever shot at. The old buck had a dressed weight of 171 pounds.

DNR Deer Researcher John Ozoga, who recently retired from the Cusino Wildlife Experiment Station at Shingleton, said the oldest wild buck he can recall is another one aged at 12 1/2 from Alger County. Ozoga was studying deer in the Petrel Grade Deer Yard at the time and he first saw the buck during late December. He said the whitetail appeared to be in rough shape and it had already shed its antlers. The deer was killed by coyotes during late February and John recovered its jaw for aging.

Arthur Goodman from Trenary shot an old buck that was estimated to be between 10 1/2 and 12 1/2 years old on November 28, 1992. He said he was hunting from a blind when the buck appeared on the edge of a swamp just before dark. Goodman dropped the whitetail at a distance of 50 yards with a .30-06.

The old buck's rack had 14 points. It had a typical 10-point frame with four nontypical points in various locations. The longest nontypical point was a long drop tine growing from the base of the second point on the left beam. The deer had huge feet and a long body, but the carcass only had a dressed weight of 162 pounds.

John Rasmussen, Jr. from Munising got another Alger County buck that proved to be 11 1/2 on November 18, 1993. Paul Friedrich at the DNR's Rose Lake Lab determined that buck's age by looking at a cross section

Arthur Goodman of Trenary with a 14-pointer from Alger County that was between 10 1/2 and 12 1/2 years old.

of a tooth. Rasmussen said he was hunting from a blind when he shot the oldtimer. He had bait in front of the blind, but he was also watching a scrape that was about 80 yards further away. The deer was checking the scrape when John saw it.

Surprisingly, that buck's teeth weren't worn as much as a whitetail of that age should have been. John said the teeth looked like those from jaws of other deer that were 5 1/2 or 6 1/2 years old. If a cross section of a tooth had not been examined, its age would have been underestimated.

The buck's antlers did reflect its age, however. John said the right antler was a big spike with a couple of knobs on it. The left beam was real thick and had four points. Rasmussen said the brow tine on the left side was in the shape of a T. The whitetail obviously had much better antlers when it was younger. The deer had a dressed weight of 184 pounds.

Another buck that beat the odds reached the age of 10 1/2 and spent his days near Rudyard in Chippewa County. This buck's age isn't all that made him special. In fact, he was special long before he became 10 years old.

Although he was a wild whitetail all of his life, this buck, which was called Bucky, developed a close relationship with a human, a human who was also a deer hunter. The man's name is Bill Mattson. He lived near Rudyard and is very much a part of Bucky's story. Bucky was on his own in the wild

Bill Mattson feeds Bucky by hand when the wild whitetail was 4 1/2 years old.

most of the year, just like any other buck, but managed to elude hunters during three months of bow and gun deer seasons, unlike many other bucks. Every winter, Bucky showed up at Bill Mattson's home and would accept food right from Bill's hands. This went on for the buck's entire life.

Bill moved to a rural setting near Rudyard during 1971. His home is surrounded by swamp where whitetails winter. As a hunter, he was interested in seeing deer and helping them to make it through the U.P.'s long, cold winters, so he started feeding them. Bucky was one of the special deer that took advantage of Bill's handouts.

The buck was born during 1974 and was first brought to Bill's yard by his mother and he returned every winter thereafter on his own. Bucky's first set of antlers had 4 points. By the time he was three, he developed 10-point antlers.

The unusual buck's rack had a typical 10-point frame throughout his life, but by the time he was 6 1/2, short nontypical points started appearing. The most points he ever had was 15 in 1983 when 9 1/2 years old. There were three short nontypical points on the right beam and two on the left.

December 24, 1984 was the last time Bill saw Bucky. A bowhunter shot the whitetail on Christmas Day. As it turned out, the quality of Bucky's rack deteriorated significantly during his last year. There were only eight major points, instead of 10, and some of them were broken off. Nonetheless, the antlers still scored 127 4/8. When at its best, I think Bucky's rack would have scored in the 140s.

Earl Hulst from Caledonia bagged another old timer in the U.P. during the 1993 deer season that was unusual in more ways than its age. The Marquette County whitetail he shot near Gwinn on opening day of gun season only had three legs and the animal was estimated to be 10 1/2 years old based on tooth wear. The buck's teeth were so badly worn, they were near the gum line.

Despite the handicap and its age, the deer was in excellent condition, according to Hulst. He said the carcass was covered with fat and the body was large. The animal had an estimated dressed weight between 160 and 170 pounds. Hulst also reported venison from the deer was excellent eating.

The left front leg was missing at the shoulder. The leg was lost at least a year earlier because the injury was perfectly healed. Hulst said a piece of hair-covered hide hung down from the shoulder where the leg had been.

While butchering the buck, the hunter found some old pieces of lead from a bullet in the fat on the lower right side of the chest, indicating the bullet that broke the leg may have gone through the lower chest cavity. It's amazing the deer survived such an injury, unless the lungs received minor damage or none at all.

The whitetail's antlers clearly showed the effects of its age and injury. The right antler, the one opposite the missing leg, was small and deformed, according to Hulst, and only had three points. The left antler was

Sault Ste. Marie taxidermist Randy Desormeau With Bucky's last rack. Notice the broken tine and blunted beam tips. The quality of the whitetail's antlers definitely declined in quality during his last years.

normally shaped and had four points, but the beam and tines were short. The buck probably had a much larger rack when it was younger.

Hulst said he shot the buck while watching a deer crossing between a pair of beaver ponds. He said the ponds tend to funnel whitetails through the thick cover where he was posted. He added that the spot is hard to get to because of water and he wore hip boots to reach the location.

Earl Hulst of Caledonia with a 3-legged Marquette County buck that was 10 1/2 years old. (Photo courtesy Earl Hulst)

"When I shot the buck, I thought he was wounded," Hulst said. "I only saw him take two steps because of the thick cover, but it looked like he was limping. He dropped instantly, but I didn't bother to walk up to him because I thought who ever wounded the deer would come along soon. There was excellent tracking conditions.

"I figured I would let the other hunter tag the deer. When nobody showed up after an hour, I decided to check the animal. I was thinking about backtracking the buck to find the hunter who wounded him. I was surprised when I discovered the buck only had three legs and it wasn't wounded. That explained why no one else showed up, so I tagged the deer."

Former Marquette resident Al Neuchterlein shot a Delta County buck on November 15, 1989 that proved to be 10 1/2 based on examination of a cross section from one of its teeth. Neuchterlein was hunting from a blind near some cedar trees that had been rubbed by a decent buck. It was late in the day when the buck appeared. There was a doe to his left and the buck came from the right and approached the doe. The whitetail's antlers had 13 points, with one odd-shaped nontypical tine growing from the base of one beam in a semi-circle.

Although bucks seldom reach their 10th birthday in Michigan, it is more common for does to reach that age. Does are less sought after by

121

hunters, have less stress associated with breeding and because of that have a better chance of surviving tough winters. The oldest doe on record for the state is probably one shot in the U.P. during November of 1967. A cross section of one of its teeth yielded an age of 19 1/2. There was no record of what county the doe came from or who the hunter was.

Lynn Dushane from Southgate also shot a doe that might have been as old during the 1989 gun season. When he had the doe checked at a DNR station at Pte. Mouillee he was told the whitetail was between 15 1/2 and 20 1/2 years old, based on tooth wear. It's too bad he didn't have them take a tooth for cross sectioning to determine its exact age. At any rate, that doe was at least 15 1/2 years old.

"She was a lone deer and in good shape when I shot her," Dushane wrote. "She dressed out at 165 pounds and her front teeth were worn down to within 1/16-inch from her gum. Her feet were split and spread out from age. For years I thought the tracks were another big buck."

Dennis Vissering of Three Lakes bagged what may be the oldest doe taken with bow and arrow in the state during the fall of 1987. That whitetail proved to be 14 1/2 years old, based on the examination of a cross section of one of the deer's teeth. Dennis arrowed the deer in southern Ontonagon County during October.

After successfully making a 22-yard shot at the doe and recovering it, Vissering discovered that its liver was full of flukes and teeth were worn to the gums. DNR Wildlife Biologist Rob Aho at Baraga examined the doe, which had a dressed weight of 104 pounds, and said it had to be at least 12 years old based on tooth wear. At the same time, Aho took a tooth from the deer for processing in the lab by Paul Friedrich. The exact age of whitetails can be determined by counting the rings in a cross section of a tooth.

Friedrich determined the doe was 14 1/2. Dennis said the deer was accompanied by a fawn at the time she was shot, so she was still producing offspring.

The DNR's John Ozoga has records of a doe that continued having fawns until 13 years old. That doe was part of a herd kept in a square mile enclosure at the research facility in Shingleton until she was almost 13 and then released in the wild. Ozoga said she gave birth to a set of twins in the wild and was shot illegally later that year.

The deer expert said does that reach 13 and 14 years of age still manage to breed normally, but not many wild whitetails live that long. The oldest doe Ozoga has records on lived in the wild all of her life and was almost 17 when he last saw her in Alger County. He initially captured and ear-tagged the doe in a winter yard as a fawn on March 10, 1955 and recaptured her in the same yard on March 12, 1969 when almost 15. Two years later, he saw her again.

Most older does manage to escape hunters, according to Ozoga, making severe winters a more important factor in their chances of survival.

Al Neuchterlein with 10 1/2-year old buck he bagged in Delta County during 1988. (Photo courtesy Jon Hayes)

The author checks out antlers on his best Michigan buck where the animal crashed into a fallen tree. It's an 11-pointer scoring 148 4/8 that was taken in Marquette County during 1990. Knowledge he has gained from interviewing hunters who have bagged Michigan's biggest bucks has made him a better big buck hunter.

Author

Richard P. Smith is an award winning outdoor writer and photographer living in Marquette, Michigan with his wife and business partner Lucy. He is a nationally recognized writer, photographer and speaker who has written 11 books and hundreds of magazine articles.

Smith's last book, the 3rd edition of <u>Michigan Big Game Records</u>, done in cooperation with Commemorative Bucks of Michigan, was published during the fall of 1993 and contains records through 1992 seasons. His other books include <u>Deer Hunting</u>, <u>Tracking Wounded Deer</u>, <u>Hunting Trophy Black Bear</u>, <u>Hunting Rabbits and Hares</u> and <u>Animal Tracks and Signs of North America</u>.

Smith is a Field Editor for Deer & Deer Hunting and Michigan Hunting and Fishing Magazines. He writes a Regional Report about Upper Peninsula happenings for Michigan Out-of-Doors Magazine and contributes to Michigan Sportsman and Woods-N-Water News. His writing and photography are used regularly in national magazines including Outdoor Life, American Hunter, Bowhunter, Petersen's Hunting, North American Hunter and North American Whitetail.

The author is a recognized expert on deer and black bear behavior and biology as well as hunting these species of big game. He has hunted deer and bear extensively in Michigan and throughout North America for more than 25 years.

Books by Richard P. Smith

DEER HUNTING (2ND EDITION) - This best selling book was so popular it was updated to include even more information and photographs. The second edition includes 260 pages and 139 photos that show and tell you all you need to know to successfully hunt whitetails and mule deer throughout North America with modern firearms, muzzleloaders, bow and arrow, and camera. There are bonus chapters on deer biology and management, hunting ethics and more. There's something in this book for you whether you are a beginner or an experienced veteran like the author. Price: $18 postpaid.

TRACKING WOUNDED DEER - Nobody likes to wound a deer, but it sometimes happens. This is the book that will help prepare you for the time when you have to follow a deer you've shot and will increase your chances of recovering wounded animals regardless of where they are hit. This book is must reading for bowhunters since trailing arrowed deer is part of every successful hunt. Eight pages of color photos show blood and hair sign never before published. There are plenty of black and white photos to go with the 160 pages of text, too. Price: $19 postpaid.

Records thru 1992
MICHIGAN BIG GAME RECORDS (1ST-3RD EDITIONS) - The 3rd edition is a bigger and better reference for Michigan hunters with the addition of turkey records. This 272-page volume continues the tradition of providing the best and latest information about trophy deer, bear and elk hunting in the state. The who, how, where and when of trophy kills from 1989-1992 are covered in the 3rd edition. Those taken from 1986-'88 are discussed in the 256-page 2nd edition and trophies taken through 1985 are covered in the 1st edition (216 pages). Each edition of the record book has different chapters about big game hunting in Michigan, with emphasis on deer, and hundreds of photos. You will want to own a set of all three books to become one of the state's most knowledgeable big game hunters.
All three editions are offered in both hard (HC) and soft(SC) cover versions. Price: Set of 3(SC) $55
        2nd &3rd Editions(SC) $21 each, 1st Edition $18
        Set of 3(HC) $113, 1st,2nd,& 3rd Editions(HC) $39 each

Reduced
HUNTING RABBITS & HARES - A 153-page soft cover book containing 130 photos. The first complete book written on the subject that tells all there is to know about hunting all species of North American rabbits and hares with shotgun, rifle, handgun, black powder arms and archery equipment. Additional chapters cover population cycles, tularemia and detailed photos show how to butcher these small game animals without cutting the body cavity open.
Price: $10 postpaid (SPECIAL PRICE, $6 OFF)

ANIMAL TRACKS AND SIGNS OF NORTH AMERICA - This softbound book has 271 pages and lots of photos. It's the first guide book including actual photos of wildlife tracks and sign rather than sketches. Bonus chapters cover aging tracks, tracking wildlife and much more.
Price: $18 postpaid.

HUNTING TROPHY BLACK BEAR - A 328-page hard cover volume with 157 photos. Information on this book's fact-filled pages tells the reader all about hunting this controversial big game animal, covering all of the bases as far as hunting techniques, guns and bows. Record book bears, hiring a guide, bear biology, management and the future for black bear and more are also covered in the text.
Price: $23 postpaid.

GREAT MICHIGAN DEER TALES - If you like reading about BIG BUCKS, you will want to read this book. It contains more solid information about Michigan's most memorable bucks than any book previously published.
If you are interested in bagging a BOOK BUCK in Michigan, studying this collection of success stories will help make it happen. There's no better way to learn than from those who have already accomplished the feat.
Price: $15.50 postpaid.

Book Order Form

Quantity   Price

_____ GREAT MICHIGAN DEER TALES ($15.50)   _____

_____ DEER HUNTING (2ND EDITION) ($18)   _____

_____ TRACKING WOUNDED DEER ($19)   _____

_____ MICHIGAN BIG GAME RECORDS
          (Specify edition & HC or SC)   _____

_____ HUNTING RABBITS & HARES ($10)   _____

_____ ANIMAL TRACKS & SIGNS OF NORTH AMERICA ($18)   _____

_____ HUNTING TROPHY BLACK BEAR ($23)   _____

                                        TOTAL PAYMENT ENCLOSED _____

Prices include postage and handling. Make checks payable to:
                                        Smith Publications

Please send U.S. funds. Canadian orders add $1/book (Parcel Post) or $3/book(Air Mail).

Rush orders add $2/book (Priority mail) or $4/book (2 day UPS) in MI, $10/book outside MI (No PO boxes). Please write RUSH on order.

Name_____

Address _____

City_____

State/Zip _____

Phone # _____

Send orders to: **Smith Publications
                814 Clark St.
                Marquette, MI 49855**